Dedicated To My Mother And Father

TABLE OF CONTENTS

TABLE OF CONTENTS

INTRODUCTION

An Historical Approach to Sociology of Law
Theory with Particular Attention to its
Evolution in the United States

The present subdivision of criminology known
as the sociology of law consists at present of
four parts: (1) sociology of civil law, (2)
sociology of criminal law, (3) sociological jurisprudence, and (4) anthropology of law.

Each part of this field evolved at different
times in Europe and the United States due to the
particular interests of those engaged in the study
of law, philosophy, or the social sciences. All
of this intellectual activity took place in the
mid to late nineteenth century.

The earliest writings that can truly be
classified as within the field of legal sociology
are those of Henry Sumner Maine who in 1861 began
the tradition of anthropology of law with the
publication of Ancient Law. This classic was
followed in 1883 with Maine's followup work,
Dissertations on Early Law and Custom. Durkheim's
work, described below, was also quite influential
to the field of anthropology of law. The earliest
American work in the area is that of William Graham
Sumner who in 1906 published a work entitled
Folkways which is only in a limited way concerned
with the anthropology of law.

The second area of the sociology of law to
evolve was sociological jurisprudence. This began
indirectly with an article written by Oliver
Wendell Holmes entitled, "The Path of the Law"
which was followed by a series of articles written
by Roscoe Pound. The first was entitled, "The
Need for a Sociological Jurisprudence" published

in 1907. This was followed by a three part article appearing in the Harvard Law Review in 1911-12
entitled, "The Scope and Purpose of Sociological
Jurisprudence" which set the stage for the evolution of American sociology of law since Pound was
influenced by both European legal philosophers as
well as American Sociologists.[1]

The sociology of criminal law was the product
of the research of Emile Durkheim who discussed
aspects of the field in his classic works, Division of Labor in Society (1893) and Suicide (1897).
This pioneer research was continued in France by
Duguit, Levy, and Hauriou in the 1920's after
Durkheim's death.[2] It was not until the mid
1950's that American theorists showed an embryonic
interest in the sociology of criminal law. A
series of articles appeared in the Journal of
Criminal Law, Criminology, and Police Science from
1954 to 1959 which restarted an interest in the
field. Gilbert Geis in 1959 wrote an article
entitled "Sociology, Criminology, and Criminal Law"
which chided criminologists for their lack of
interest in the field of sociology of criminal law.

The last area of sociology of law to evolve
was the sociology of civil law. It began with a
book published in 1904 by Karl Renner entitled
The Institutions of Private Law. This work was
largely ignored in academic circles due to its
socialist orientation. Thus it was not until 1913
that another Austrian named Eugen Ehrlich published
his Fundamental Principles of the Sociology of Law
that the sociology of civil law was formulated in
its basic outline. This book was extensively
utilized by Max Weber in his writings on sociology
of law, the notes of which eventually became Law
in Economy and Society published in 1922 after
Weber's death. It was not until 1945 that an
American theorist examined the sociology of civil
law. This was Roscoe Pound in his review of the

field entitled, "Sociology of Law" that appeared in an edited text, Twentieth Century Sociology.

So much for a brief history of the foundations of the four parts of the body of knowledge known as the sociology of law. Let us turn to an analysis of the advancement of the field from the decade of the 1920's until the present day.

Sociology of Law - 1920's

The 1920's was not a productive period for theory building in both Europe and America. There were no significant publications in either sociology of criminal law or sociological jurisprudence even taking into consideration the writings of Duguit, Levy, Hauriou, and Cardozo. In the sociology of civil law two publications appeared in 1922, Weber's book, Law in Economy and Society and Ehrlich's article, "The Sociology of Law". Both theorists had died before publication of their respective works. Anthropology of law publications were also limited to the work of Bronislaw Malinowski and Robert Lowie. The former published his masterpiece, Crime and Custom in Savage Society in 1926 and the latter Primitive Society in 1920 and "Anthropology and Law" in 1927.

The lack of significant theoretical data being published in this decade is due in part to the fact that sociology as a field was moving away from both criminology and jurisprudence in an attempt to establish itself as a legitimate discipline. There was also the fact that most theory building had been European in origin and with the deaths of both Weber and Ehrlich there was a void created by lack of direction to the field. Americans in particular did not accept the challenge of Pound for close cooperation between law professors and sociologists so nothing significant evolved in either criminal law theory or jurisprudence

areas.[3] Finally anthropology was at the stage of
growth where it was not in a position as yet to
test either Malinowski or Lowie as to their generalizations concerning the legal institution in
traditional society.[4] The growth of anthropology
of law theory was hindered by the bitter controversy that raged between Radcliffe-Brown and
Malinowski during the 1920's and 1930's over whose
viewpoint was correct.[5]

Sociology of Law - 1930's

The decade of the thirties saw for the most
part a continuation of general disinterest in the
sociology of law field. Sociology of criminal law
theory still was an intellectual wasteland even
though Edwin Sutherland recognized its existence
as early as 1936.[6] Sociological jurisprudence
also experienced a very limited output as only two
articles of value appeared. The first was Robert
Angell's "The Value of Sociology to Law" in 1933
and Moses Aronson's tribute to Cardozo entitled,
"Cardozo's Doctrine of Sociological Jurisprudence"
published in 1938.

In the area of sociology of civil law, Georges
Gurvitch as general secretary of the International
Institute of Sociology of Law (Paris, 1931-1940)
was active in the publication of both the Archives
de Sociologie Juridique and the Annuaires des
Congres. Huntington Cairns published his book, Law
and the Social Sciences in 1935 which dealt with
both sociology and anthropology. Finally Nicholus
Timasheff published, An Introduction to the Sociology of Law in 1939. All these publications had
little influence and impact on American theory
since they were oriented toward a European
audience.

Huntington Cairns wrote an article in 1931
entitled, "Law and Anthropology" which was later

expanded in his 1935 text, Law and the Social
Sciences. The lengthy controversy in anthropology
of law between Radcliffe-Brown and Malinowski was
heightened by the former's essay published in 1933
on "Primitive Law" and the latter's indirect reply
appearing as the introduction to Herbert Hogbin's
book, Law and Order in Polynesia in 1934. This
intellectual rivalry continued to retard the
advancement of the field for the remainder of the
decade with the exception of the work of Arthur
Diamond. He published a significant book as a
partial refutation and clarification of Maine's
classic entitled Primitive Law in 1935. Unfortunately American anthropological theory remained
dormant during this time.

Sociology of Law - 1940's

The 1940's due in part to the demands of the
Second World War showed a continued lack of progress in the advancement of the sociology of law.
Sociology of criminal law and sociological jurisprudence continued to provide no new insights into
further advancement of theory. This was despite
the fact that Sutherland was influenced by the
writings of Jerome Hall who was oriented toward
the analysis of societal legal processes. The
preoccupation of theorists typified by Sutherland
in dealing with crime control (i.e., criminal
behavior) prevented them from investigating the
evolution of criminal law in society.[7]

Georges Gurvitch in 1941 published an article
entitled, "Major Problems of the Sociology of Law"
which became the model for his text which appeared
in 1947, Sociology of Law. The significance of
this book was not in Gurvitch's theory of law
which was more philosophical than sociological
(i.e., akin to today's phenomenological approach)
but his thorough critique of the field's theorists

from the eighteenth century to the 1940's. Roscoe
Pound wrote an article in 1945, "The Sociology of
Law" which was a broad update of his 1911-12
historical analysis of theory building. This
enhanced the historical orientation of part of the
Gurvitch book but did not advance the state of
sociology of civil law theory.

Only in the area of anthropology of law arose
definite contributions to theory during the decade.
This was the work of Karl Llewellyn and E. Adamson
Hoebel in 1941, The Cheyenne Way: Conflict and
Case Law in Primitive Jurisprudence and Hoebel's
article, "Law and Anthropology" published in 1946.
Hoebel in his work was influenced by the juris-
prudence of Llewellyn which finally advanced
anthropology of law theory past the Radcliffe-
Brown / Malinowski controversy.

Sociology of Law - 1950's

The decade of the Fifties showed a definite
movement toward theory building in the field.
Although the sociology of civil law only had one
contribution, that of Timasheff, "Growth and Scope
of Sociology of Law", 1957, there was considerable
progress made indirectly due to the translation
into English of Weber's work by Rheinstein (Law in
Economy and Society) in 1954. Thus American
theorists could now examine Weber and tie his work
to that of Ehrlich, Gurvitch, Timasheff, and
Renner. The stage was now set for a definite
American contribution to the field based on a
solid European foundation.

The sociology of criminal law advanced drama-
tically with the publication throughout the Fifties
of a series of articles in the Journal of Criminal
Law, Criminology, and Police Science. First to
appear in 1954 by Margaret Vine was an article on

xii

Gabriel Tarde. Next to appear in 1955 was an
article by Gilbert Geis on Jeremy Bentham followed in the same year by an article on Cesare
Beccaria by Elio Monachesi. In 1956 Manuel
Lopez-Rey published an article on Pedro Montero
which was followed by Walter Lunden's work on
Emile Durkheim in 1958. The series of articles
was completed in 1959 with the publication of
C. Ray Jeffery's "The Historical Development of
Criminology". Thus the Journal of Criminal Law,
Criminology, and Police Science managed to create
a definite interest in the major theorists of
sociology of criminal law with their concise
articles dealing with the classic period of
European theory building.

Two other notable publications complete our
review of the 1950's. In 1958 appeared the book
Theoretical Criminology by George Vold that
anticipated the conflict theory approach to the
sociology of criminal law. In 1959 Gilbert Geis
wrote his article, "Sociology, Criminology, and
Criminal Law" that became the theme for the area
in the 1960's.

Jerome Hall published his classic text,
Theft, Law and Society in 1952 which brought sociological jurisprudence in the United States into
modern form. This was the type of study advocated
in 1907 by Roscoe Pound but somehow never attempted
until the 1950's. Lastly Hans Zeisel wrote an
update of the progress of sociological jurisprudence entitled "Sociology of Law, 1945-1955" in
1956.

The modern classic for the field of anthropology of law was written in 1954 by E. Adamson
Hoebel entitled The Law of Primitive Man. This book
was the culmination of theoretical efforts from
both Malinowski and Lowie. It placed anthropological theory in perspective since it utilized both

ethnographic and jurisprudential orientations.
This book was preceded by Arthur Diamond's
second book, The Evolution of Law and Order in
1951 which was an update of his earlier work in
the same theoretical framework as Maine. Thus it
is to Hoebel that contemporary anthropology of law
owes a debt of gratitude.

Sociology of Law - 1960's

The sociology of law as a discipline came into
maturity in this decade in America. It is as if
all previous theoretical efforts finally paid off.
Both American and European theorists made definite
contributions to all areas of this subdivision of
criminology. Twenty books, one journal, and
twenty-seven articles appeared during the decade.
It was as if sociological theorists had rediscov-
ered the legal institution and nothing had previously been written on the topic. In fact there was
a backing away from research on criminal etiology
coupled with a curiosity about the origins of crime
in society that brought about the reinterest in the
field that had more or less lay dormant since the
end of the first decade of the twentieth century in
American social theory. This reinterest was helped
by both Federal and private foundation funds which
were used to encourage both law professors and
criminologists to study and teach courses on the
evolution of law in society.[8]

Geoffrey Sawer of Australia edited a book of
original essays entitled, Studies in the Sociology
of Law in 1961 which began the contemporary interest in sociology of civil law. The following year
two significant books of original essays were
published in the United States. F. James Davis'
Society and the Law and William Evan's Law and
Sociology. These three edited books of essays did
more to advance the field than many previous writings. In 1963 Vilhelm Aubert wrote an article

"Researches in the Sociology of Law" which was
European in orientation. Richard Schwartz and
James Miller in 1964 added a cross-cultural per-
spective in their essay "Legal Evolution and
Societal Complexity".

It was in 1965 that Geoffrey Sawer wrote his
Anglo-Australian text, Law in Society. This was
followed by Jerome Skolnick's editorship of the
Law and Society supplement of the journal Social
Problems and his lead article "The Sociology of
Law in America: Overview and Trends". All this
writing and reviewing of sociology of civil law
research led to the creation of the Law and
Society Review in 1966. This new journal published two articles in its first volume that added
intellectual stimulus to the field. First appeared Carl Auerbach's "Legal Tasks for the Sociologist" followed by Jerome Skolnick's "Social Research on Legality: A Reply to Auerbach". In
separate developments the same year Jack Gibbs
published an article, "The Sociology of Law and
Normative Phenomena" and Treves published La
Sociologia del Diritto in Italy.

The year 1968 saw a number of books and
articles make their appearance in the field.
Edwin Schur published Law and Society: A Sociological View, the first introductory text on the
topic and Rita Simon came out with a book of
readings entitled The Sociology of Law. Julien
Freund published his The Sociology of Max Weber
which included an analysis and interpretation at
the basic level of Weber's sociology of law.
Arnold Rose also wrote "Law and the Cause of Social
Problems". Another major advance for the field was
the appearance of two articles in the International
Encyclopedia of the Social Sciences. Philip
Selznick wrote the article "The Sociology of Law"
and Paul Bohannon the article "Law and Legal Institutions". These articles updated and attempted to

define the scope and needs of the sociology of
law field since the 1930's when the first Encyclopedia of the Social Sciences was published.

Vilhelm Aubert published his edited work
Sociology of Law in 1969 which was much like the
previously published anthology of Simon. Lawrence
Friedman and Stuart Macaulay added a third text
Law and the Behavioral Sciences the same year
followed by Daniel Swett's "Cultural Bias in the
American Legal System" and Alice Tay's "Law in
Communist China, I and II".

Thus the sociology of civil law saw the rise
of new theoretical studies, anthologies, interpretations of old theories, social problems analysis of the legal institution, and cross-cultural
comparisons. Most importantly the decade saw the
rise of an American journal, Law and Society
Review, which dealt explicitly with the sociology
of law.

The sociology of criminal law showed some
signs of intellectual vitality in the 1960's but
not as much activity as in the civil law area.
C. Ray Jeffery wrote an essay "Criminal Justice
and Social Change" in 1962 which essentially was
a structural-functional perspective. This same
perspective was used by both Chambliss and Schur
in their respective books in 1969. The former
wrote an extensive work Crime and the Legal
Process and the latter wrote on overlegislation of
crimes in Our Criminal Society. Richard Quinney
in an essay, "Toward A Sociology of Criminal Law"
began the theoretical shift toward use of conflict
theory which was followed by Austin Turk in his
book Criminality and Legal Order.

Sociological jurisprudence also experienced
its largest production of data. The year 1961
saw the publication of H. L. A. Hart's The Concept

of Law and E. K. Braybrooke's essay "The Sociological Jurisprudence of Roscoe Pound". These were followed in 1962 by Karl Llewellyn's essay on sociological jurisprudence in his book Jurisprudence and Adam Podgorecki's article "Law and Social Engineering". In 1964 Gilbert Geis wrote "Sociology and Sociological Jurisprudence: Admixture of Law and Lore" which was an update of the field in a style similar to Pound's earlier call for cooperation between the two disciplines. Francis Allen wrote The Borderland of Criminal Justice: Essays in Law and Criminology. Finally Lon Fuller wrote The Morality of Law which was in part a critique of Hart.

Harold Berman and William Greiner published The Nature and Functions of Law in 1966 followed by Julius Stone's Law and the Social Sciences which was written in the tradition of Pound and Llewellyn. Lawrence Friedman added two significant articles in 1967 and 1969, the former titled, Legal Rules and the Process of Social Change" and the latter "Legal Culture and Social Development".

The anthropology of law began the 1960's with an essay by J. A. Barnes "Law as Politically Active: An Anthropological View" (1961). Harry Ball and George Simpson in 1962 wrote "Law and Social Change: Sumner Reconsidered". This was followed in 1964 by Paul Bohannon's "Anthropology and the Law" and Robert Redfield's "Primitive Law". Both articles were historical reviews of theory.

In 1965 The Ethnology of Law special supplement under the editorship of Laura Nader appeared in the American Anthropologist. Thus anthropology of law theorists made the same attempt as sociology of law theorists to create a definite pulling together of the field along with providing some direction for future growth. Paul Bohannon presented his latest theoretical approach in his

article, "The Differing Realms of the Law" which
in part is similar to Barnes' earlier essay.
Leopold Pospisil in a 1968 essay, "Law and Order"
attempted to review the contributions of both
European and American theorists and create his own
theory of legal evolution in traditional societies.
This was followed by Max Gluckman's essay "Concepts in the Comparative Study of Tribal Law" that
appeared in Laura Nader's edited text Law in Culture and Society that was published in 1969.

Sociology of Law - 1970's

The 1970's began with the publication of two
edited reference books in the sociology of civil
law, William Chambliss and Robert Seidman,
Sociology of Law: A Research Bibliography and
Richard Schwartz and Jerome Skolnick, Society and
the Legal Order, both 1970. These texts were
followed in 1971 with the Jon Sutherland and
Michael Werthman edited book Comparative Concepts
of Law and Order. A Portuguese theorist M.E. Brito
came out in 1972 with his Sociology of Law: A
Selected Bibliography followed in 1973 by N.
Herpin's Les Sociologues Americians et Le Siecle.
Thus the first few years of the decade produced
extensive reference material that was also cross-
cultural in nature.

The British Journal of Law and Society came
out in 1974 which showed the growing interest in
the field abroad. Upendra Baxi published an
article, "Durkheim and Legal Evolution: Some
Problems of Disproof-Rejoinder". There also appeared the same year Clive Grace and Philip
Wilkinson's, "Social Action as a Methodology for
the Sociology of Law".

The year 1975 saw the publication of the
edited text by Ronald Akers and Richard Hawkins,
Law and Control in Society. This was followed by

V. Pocar's reference work, La Sociologia del
Diritto Negli Anni 60, Saggio Bibliografico.
Martin Albrow wrote, "Legal Positivism and Bourgeois Materialism: Max Weber's View of the Sociology of Law".

Donald Black published his text The Behavior
of Law along with an edited work with Maureen
Mileski entitled The Social Organization of Law
in 1976. Lynn McDonald published The Sociology of
Law and Order in Canada. There were also two books
by Treves, La Sociologia del Diritto and
L'Insegnamento Sociologico del Diritto. This was
followed by the publication of Robert Unger's
Law in Modern Society: Toward a Criticism of
Social Theory. The edited readers and texts of
1976 finally brought forth some new theorizing
concerning the sociology of civil law although
still structural-functionalist in orientation.
They were supplemented by the professional society
presentations of Robert Rich and Harold Pepinsky.
The former suggested using a paradigmatic approach
to the field in his "Sociology of Law: Toward A
Paradigmatic Perspective" while the latter presented "Anarchist-Communism as an Alternative to Due
Process". Finally Austin Turk wrote "Law as a
Weapon in Social Conflict". Thus the field began
to show an interest in both the radical/conflict
and paradigm approaches. The year 1977 waits with
anticipation the publication of Lawrence Friedman's
text, Society and the Legal System and the first
issue of the journal Law and Human Behavior.

The sociology of criminal law began the '70's
with a traditional structural-functionalist essay
by Jack Gibbs "Crime and the Sociology of Law".
This was followed in subsequent years by a rash of
books and articles for the most part from the
radical/conflict perspective. William Chambliss
and Robert Seidman wrote Law, Order, and Power in
1971 and Stuart Hills also published Crime, Power,

and Morality: The Criminal Law Process in the
United States.

William Chambliss in 1973 came out with his
Functional and Conflict Theories of Crime which
set the stage for a new radical approach to sociology of criminal law. In 1974 appeared two books
that sounded the call for serious reappraisal of
the field, Richard Quinney's "A Critical Theory of
Criminal Law" in his reader Criminal Justice in
America and Charles Reasons' "Law and the Making
of Criminals" in his reader The Criminologist:
Crime and the Criminal.

It was William Chambliss again who continued
the radical perspective of theory building with
his 1975 edited publication of Criminal Law In
Action and his 1976 edited work in collaboration
with Milton Mankoff, Whose Law: What Order? This
was followed by Harold Pepinsky's Crime and Conflict: A Study of Law and Society. Next appeared
Robert Rich's presentation, "From Renner to
Reasons: An Analysis of Radical Theories of Criminology".

Finally in 1976 appeared two essays dealing
with the paradigmatic approach to sociology of
criminal law. Charles Reasons' article "Social
Thought and Social Structure: Competing Paradigms
in Criminology" and Robert Rich's presentation,
"The Sociology of Criminal Law: Toward a Paradigmatic Perspective". Both works attempted to make
order out of the myriad of theoretical positions
put forth in the field since its birth with the
writings of Bentham, Beccaria, and Durkheim until
its resurrection with the writings of Turk, Quinney,
and Chambliss.

Elliot Currie lead off the theorizing in
sociological jurisprudence in the '70's with his

article in 1971, "Sociology of Law: the Unasked
Questions". This was followed in 1972 by Donald
Black's article, "The Boundries of Legal Soci-
ology". J. Carbonnier came out with his text,
Sociologie Juridique the same year.

In 1974 Jack Ladinsky prepared "The Teaching
of Law and Social Science Courses in the United
States" which was a review of the efforts to
promote sociological jurisprudence in law schools
in America from the time of Roscoe Pound to the
early 1970's. In 1975 Robert Rich presented a
paper entitled "Sociological Jurisprudence:
Toward a Paradigmatic Perspective". Lastly in
1976 two articles appeared in the same issue of
Law and Society Review, Malcolm Feeley's "The
Concept of Laws in Social Science: a Critique and
Notes on an Expanded View" and Philippe Nonet's
"For Jurisprudential Sociology". Thus sociological
jurisprudence in the 1970's has remained almost
untouched by the intellectual movement from utilization of structural-functionalist theory to
conflict theory.

Anthropology of law in the 1970's appears to
have shown an intellectual lack of interest in
moving ahead from its traditional structural-
functionalist approach in theory building. Only
three works of merit have appeared to date.
Stanley Diamond's "The Rule of Law Versus the Order
of Custom" in 1971, Henkin's "Law and Disorder
Around the World: Other People's Problems", and
Robert Rich's "The Anthropology of Law: Toward a
Paradigmatic Perspective". Thus the field has
placed itself in the theoretical position of ignor-
ing changes that have taken place in other areas of
this subdivision of criminology, notably the soci-
ologies of civil and criminal law.

Notes to Introduction

1 Gilbert Geis, "Sociology and Sociological Jurisprudence: Admixture of Law and Lore", Kentucky Law Journal 52 (Winter, 1964) 267-277.

2 Georges Gurvitch, Sociology of Law, London: Routledge and Kegan Paul, 1947, 96-116.

3 Gilbert Geis, op. cit., 52: 267-277.

4 Marvin Harris, The Rise of Anthropological Theory, New York: Crowell, 1968, Chapters 13 and 19.

5 Ibid., 545-556.

6 Karl Schuessler (ed.) Edwin H. Sutherland: On Analyzing Crime, Chicago: University of Chicago Press, 1973, xxv-xxx.

7 Ibid., xxx-xxxiii.

8 Jack Ladinisky, The Teaching of Law and Social Science Courses in the United States, Working Paper number 11, Center For Law and Behavioral Science, Madison, Wisconsin: University of Wisconsin, 1974.

Chapter I

Sociology of Civil Law

Eugen Ehrlich

Ehrlich in his book, Fundamental Principles of the Sociology of Law states that legal usages (i.e., law facts), legal propositions (i.e., facts with reference to legal origin and effect), and all social forces which lead to law creation should be of interest to the sociologist of law. Further he feels that both the history of legal institutions and the results of practical juristic science serve as the basic subject matter for the sociology of law. The social and economic institutions of society constitute the basis of its legal life upon which juristic science rests.[1]

The foremost function of the sociology of law is to present the common elements in societal legal relations without reference to the positive law that governs them and to study the legal elements peculiar to each relation with reference to their causes and effects. Ehrlich feels that the law is based on human relations which are independent of legal propositions. Thus sociology of law concepts apply to all legal systems since the same terminology, nomenclature, and principles of arrangement apply in general to all legal systems.[2]

Ehrlich feels that legal propositions do not present a complete picture of societal law since they represent contemporary legal needs, lack continuity with the legal past, and do not consider customary law. Thus he disagrees that all law is found in legal propositions since the latter are found in the statutes.[3]

1

The concept of the "living law" is created by Ehrlich. It dominates contemporary life and is independent of legal propositions. The "living law" exists in legal documents and can be observed in the transactions of daily commerce, customs and usages, and in all associational activities. Thus the "living law" consists of concrete legal usages, relations of legal domination, legal relations, contracts, articles of association, and dispositions by last will and testament. These legal usages are the basis for the rules which regulate men's conduct, and from these rules the norms for court decisions arise from which statutory provisions arise. Therefore the "living law" constitutes the foundation of the legal order of society as well as influencing the norms for decision upon which statute law is based.[4]

The sociology of law must observe the distinction between statute law and "living law". Thus the sociology of law must investigate both societal as well as state law contributions in order to understand the contemporary state of the law. The actual influence of the state upon social law (i.e., family relations) is also important for sociological investigators.[5]

In an article entitled "The Sociology of Law", Ehrlich traces the origin and growth of legal provisions (i.e., an instrument framed in words addressed to courts as how best to decide legal cases or addressed to administrative officials how best to deal with cases). Legal provisions come into existence through judicial pronouncements or through jurisprudence. Every developed legal system has passed through a period in which legal provisions were put forth.[6]

Ehrlich states that legal provisions are dependent upon society both for its existence

and for its content. Legal provisions are created by high court decisions. Thus they are
inadequate for new legal situations because it
takes time until enough legal disputes concerning
legal provisions reach the decision-making
stage.[7]

Most law arises immediately in society on a
spontaneous basis. All law is not created by the
state through its statutes. State law (i.e., law
created through legislation) includes the laws
dealing with state functions and the constitution,
and consists of rules of administration and rules
for decision. The state is older than the law
according to Ehrlich. Thus laws are generally
formulated only after societal conflicts of
interest become so devisive that state interference is necessary[8] Law therefore is viewed as
a societal function.

Partridge in an essay entitled, "Ehrlich's
Sociology of Law" feels that the latter's most
important sociological principle of law is expressed in the fact that the center of legal
development lies in society proper, not in legislation, jurisprudence, or in judicial decision-
making. Sanctions derived from one's position in
the community rather than legal sanctions protect
our normal daily interpersonal relationships.
Law is usually enacted for the purposes of ordering activities, protecting and delimiting interests, and resolving conflicts which have already
been established within the normal functioning of
associations and organizations.[9]

Ehrlich is opposed to the identification of
law with command and is thus against the commands of a sovereign or the state (i.e., the
Austinian view) according to Partridge. He
neither equates law with legal propositions nor
attaches great importance to legal propositions.

Ehrlich's general theory of law is controversial
in its account of the relations between living
law and the rest of law, in particular the function of lawyer's law in the social control system.[10]

His conception of the sociology of law is
that main varieties of law can be treated together and consequently form part of a single
legal system. Sociology of law tasks identify
the main types of law that exist within any
society; show how the different legal levels are
interconnected; and demonstrate how each legal
level connects or interacts with the systems of
activity or relations that constitute societal
social life.[11]

The whole body of law consists of three
strata according to Partridge's interpretation of
Ehrlich. These are (1) the living law (i.e., the
rules, norms, or codes which develop by practice
or usage within the many associations of which
society is composed, and which regulate the relationships of members of associations to one
another); (2) norms for decision (i.e., those
rules, criteria, or norms which are employed by
courts in adjudicating legal conflicts); and (3)
legal propositions (i.e., the precise, universally binding formulation of the legal precept).
These three strata of law are not exclusive as
living law can exist in society before the appearance of the other two types; norms for decision can be independent of legal propositions,
while the latter have evolved from norms for
decision.[12]

Ehrlich states that law consists of the
rules, etc. which actually order or regulate a
society. Specifically it is the rules which
constitute the inner ordering of associations
that mainly regulate society (i.e., the living
law). The social control system consists of the

rules of lawyer's law coupled functionally with
the rules of living law. The development of legal
institutions is the key to discovery of the
sources of societal law.[13]

Living law is closely associated with the
functioning of associations. Associational law
contains an internal law source which evolves out
of its functioning. The interaction of members
of an association produces its rules and norms,
relations of domination and subordination, and
rights and duties (i.e., associations create
their own legal norms and legal relationships
that differ from norms of morality). Thus associations and their living law constitute the
center of societal legal development by producing
norms and institutions as "legal" as the norms
and institutions produced by the state and the
jurisprudence field. Associations according to
Ehrlich continue to evolve their own structure
despite the legislative, judicial, and litiga-
tional controls that society imposes on all
associations. This is not true since societal
controls eventually create new types of legal
relations within and between all associations.[14]

The most important function of the sociology
of law to Ehrlich is to separate those portions of
the law that regulate, order, and determine society from the norms for decision as the latter
control judicial behavior, not the normal behavior,
of members of society. Thus norms for decision
and legal propositions are subsidiary to living
law and legal relations. The latter consist of
usage, domination, possession, contract, and
testamentary disposition and are created by
society, not by legal propositions.[15]

Partridge has constructed a model representing Ehrlich's conception of the legal system
which resembles two concentric rings. The inner
ring (i.e., first legal order) refers to the

core of social relationships, transactions,
usages, norms, and rules which have arisen in
society. This is the living law or inner order
of associations. The outer ring (i.e., second
legal order) is the system of legal conceptions,
norms for decision, rules or legal propositions
created by courts or legislative bodies. The
model illustrates the diversity of relationships
between first and second legal orders and emphasizes the independence of the first legal order
(i.e., norms of ordinary life) from the second
legal order (i.e., norms known to and applied by
the lawyer).[16]

Criticism of Ehrlich's work is made by
Partridge who feels that Ehrlich's model has had
little influence on the sociology of law since it
is a sociological truism. Ehrlich's main weakness
is his lack of a hypothesis concerning the structure or mode of development of a legal system.
The basis of Ehrlich's legal system is the typical societal association whose internal structure
depends on the living law but is also effected by
legal propositions and norms for decision (i.e.,
supplemented, modified, and abolished). State law
requires associations to conform to its regulations which effectively place associations under
societal controls, which is inconsistent with
Ehrlich's model according to Partridge.[17]

The distinctive feature of Ehrlich's legal
system is the emphasis placed on societal associations and their internal structure. He was
oriented toward a social order where associations
created their own social controls (i.e., early
20th century) whereas the contemporary social
order increasingly allows state legislation to
apply social controls. Consequently his model of
a legal system is misleading since associations
(i.e., the first legal order cannot be the focus

of the source, authority, and functioning of the
law in general.[18]

Ehrlich's contribution to sociology of law
was the attempt to distinguish different types of
legal norms and legal rules. His interest centered in the social and legal role of the social
law concept (i.e., living law). He thought of
sociology of law as an accumulation of many,
diverse studies of social processes and institutions which were related to one or another of the
many different types of law.[19]

Max Weber

Weber in his work Law In Economy and Society
shows that his interest in law focused on the
problem and process of legal thought or the judicial process. He did not develop a systematic
sociology of law but he did formulate a scheme of
ideal type categories whereby the great variety of
kinds of legal thought as found in the world's
legal systems can be understood. Weber shows that
the entire character of a legal system is dominated by the kind of honoratiores that are present
(i.e., priests, judges, bureaucrats, consultants
of temporal or sacred learning, etc.).[20]

Legal thought as it appears in law making and
law finding can approximate or constitute combina-
tions of any one of a number of ideal types. Law
making and law finding can be rational or irrational either with respect to formal or to substantive criteria. In other words, they can be
guided or not guided by general rules. Weber
explains irrationality of formal and substantive
kinds and rationality of substantive and formal
kinds. The latter can be either extrinsically
or logically rational.[21]

The main sociology of law problem for Weber
concerns the determination of the relationship
between formal rationality in legal thought and
modern capitalism. He developes four postulates
that apply only to the logically formal rationality type of legal system (i.e., Western civilization). He also develops four categories of economic conduct of which modern capitalism typifies
purposely rational conduct. Weber's categories
of legal thought are parallel to his categories of
economic conduct. Modern capitalism is oriented
toward profit and rational choice of the means
conducive to that purpose. The logically formal
rationality of legal thought is the counterpart to
the purposive rationality of economic conduct.
Thus formal rationality in legal thought contributed more to the rise of capitalism than vice
versa according to Weber.[22]

Weber defines law as an order that is guaranteed by the likelihood that (physical or psychological) coercion, aiming at bringing about
conduct in conformity with the order or at aveng-
ing its violation, will be exercised by a staff of
people especially holding themselves ready for
this purpose. His definition of law is positivistic and somewhat Austinian but law is not the
command of anyone, let alone the command of the
sovereign to Weber. He views law as an order
system. Thus law is an order (i.e., set of ought
ideas held in the minds of certain people) if that
guarantee of obedience is due to the existence of
an enforcement staff of a social group.[23]

His definition of law is broad and covers
such phenomena as ecclesiastical law, gang law,
law merchant, international law, and primitive
law. Weber deals at length with the fields of
substantive law. He defines the public law and
private law concepts, right-granting law and
regulations; government and administrative law;
criminal and tort laws; deals with the concept of

imperium (i.e., punitive reactions of the master toward his group whether domestic, military, or religious); deals with the concepts of limitation and separation of powers; and deals with the concepts of substantive law and procedure.[24]

Freund in his book, The Sociology of Max Weber states that Weber studied the influence of politics, religion, and economics on the development of law in order to prove law's contribution to the rationalization peculiar to Western civilization. According to Freund, Weber's sociology of law aims at understanding the meaningful behavior of group members in relation to the laws in force and to determine the nature of the belief in their validity or in the order which they have been established. Further his legal sociology attempts to determine the extent to which the law rules are observed, and how people orient their behavior in relation to these rules. The sociology of law attempts to determine what effect a rule of law has on the social activities of individuals.[25]

Weber saw the possibility of different approaches to law in terms of whether one was suggesting the establishment of a regulation designed to protect a particular general interest, or interpreting or applying the provisions it contains, or deliberately seeking to infringe it, or complying with it in terms of its generally accepted meaning.[26]

The existence of a general apparatus of coercion is essential for Weber's sociological definition of law. This coercive apparatus includes court law, family law, organizational law, as well as canon law.[27]

His sociology of law is based on four distinctions (i.e., private and public law; positive and natural law; objective and subjective law;

and formal and material law). He states further
that there are four ideal types of law. These are
(1) irrational and material law (decisions made
purely on emotional values with no reference to
any norms); (2) irrational and formal law (decisions based on revelation or oracle); (3) rational
and material law (decisions based on ideology or
policy of a conqueror); and (4) rational and
formal law (decisions based on abstract concepts
of jurisprudence).[28]

The ideal typical development (non-chronol-
ogical) of law from a theoretical point of view is
presented by Weber. The general development of
law and legal procedure passes through a number
of stages. These are (1) charismatic legal
revelation through law profits, (2) empirical
creation and law finding by legal honoratiores,
(3) imposition of law by secular or theocratic
powers, and (4) systematic elaboration of law
and professionalized administration of justice by
persons who have received their legal training in
a learned and formally logical manner.[29]

Stoljar in an essay entitled, "Weber's
Sociology of Law" states that Weber is concerned
with the basic constituents of social order
(i.e., normative order), in particular with social
conduct which is defined as the personal acts or
omissions that directly or indirectly affect
other persons. Weber identifies and defines a
number of types of social conduct. These are
usages (i.e., regular actions that are based on
habits); customs (i.e., long familiar usages
which are pursued without thinking of any duty and
as a matter of convenience); and conventions
(i.e., customs not only in general use but ones
carrying social disapproval in case of breach or
deviation).[30]

A positive, semi-Austinian conception of law
is held by Weber. He creates a continuum at one
end of which is placed social usage and custom
(i.e., the regularities of conduct) and at the
other end is placed social convention and law
(i.e., the rules of conduct). Convention and law
differ with respect to their coercive structure
as a conventional order lacks what a legal order
has (i.e., a specialized staff for implementing
coercive power). An order requires a general
pattern of obedience, and Weber is interested in
identifying the types of motives which will reflect different normative orders.[31]

A central theme in Weber's sociology of law
is his analysis of the concept of domination. He
feels that the coercive apparatus of the state is
an empirical expression of the phenomena of
domination. Domination is defined as the probability that certain commands will be obeyed by a
definable group of people. There are three types
of legitimate domination: (1) charismatic (i.e.,
the heroic or extraordinary force in an individual
which attracts and holds obedience on the part of
others); (2) traditional (i.e., acceptance of
authority due to old customs or a sacred tradition); and (3) rational (i.e., a conscious,
rational system which bestows legality upon the
commands of certain people provided both the
commands and commanders comply with the conditions
designated by the system). The first two types of
domination are based on a belief for a personal
order while the last type of domination rests
upon respect for an impersonal order.[32]

The distinction between domination by virtue
of monopolistic power (i.e., corporate influence
upon society) and domination by virtue of the
exercise of patriarchal, magisterial, or princely
power (i.e., no formal choice of freedom) is made
by Weber. He uses the concept of imperium to

describe the power of princes, magistrates, and bureaucratic officials. Weber shows that in reforming and replacing already existing law, imperium represents a movement away from sacred, magical forms of law-making to a rational form of law creation.[33]

His theory of legal growth presents the categorization of the major developmental stages of law and their sociological structure. Weber's central distinction is that between rational and irrational laws, a distinction that tends to explain that law does not historically require the existence of general rules though it does require a setting of domination and adjudication (i.e., at first charismatic domination through priests followed by a gradual movement toward tradition which may become transformed into a rational order).[34]

Weber's sociology of law can be divided into three areas according to Stoljar. These are (1) the normative order (definition of law, etc.); (2) the stages of legal growth; and (3) the impact of professional lawyers on society.[35]

Karl Renner

Renner's book, The Institutions of Private Law utilizes the Marxist system to deal with the sociology of law. In particular he deals with the impact of economic forces and social change upon the functioning of legal institutions. Renner is concerned with private law legal institutions such as land ownership, movable property, law of contract, mortgage and lease, and marriage and succession. His sociology of law does not deal with the social forces which bring about the creation of legal norms, and changes in the positive law. Further his theory does not

investigate the problem of the origin and evolution of legal principles at a given stage of
societal development since Renner presumes the
stability and relative immutability of legal
institutions such as property and contract.[36]

He was a positivist and viewed the legal
norm as indifferent towards its social function.
Renner adheres to the view that every norm is an
imperative (i.e., never more than a command
addressed by one individual to another). Further
he feels that the law can never fully control
social groups or organizations although law may
enhance their efficiency. The conception of law
as a series of imperatives is central to his
sociology of law.[37]

Changes in the economy are often the result
of legal developments though it is more usual to
find that a change in the economic system usually
produces changes in the legal system. Legislation
is viewed as a response of the law to changes
which have already taken place in the social and
economic institutions of society. Renner states
that a change in the economy never occurs without
political changes and usually only after a time
lag of many years. Economic societal ends can
only be achieved through the simultaneous operation of many legal institutions in capitalist
society. Law's economic function is its sub-
servience to the economic process while its
social function is its use as a tool in the
maintenance of the socio-economic processes of
production and reproduction of societal institutions (i.e., maintenance of societal status
quo).[38]

Society to Renner is a dialectical process
which considers its legal institution as a rigid
abstract of interrelated imperatives. The dis-
crepancy between the normative content of the law
(i.e., static) and its economic and social

function (i.e., dynamic) is the key to the law's
dialectical development. The social function of
law keeps society organized. Thus law aids in
keeping societal production and reproduction
operating; aids in establishing a societal
hierarchy of subordination; and helps with societal distribution of the handling and possessing
of goods among societal members.[39]

Capitalist society prevents the dialectical
process from running its course through its pre-
tense of being able to forego a functional organization of possession and labor. Capitalist
society created a legal system which stressed the
will of the individual over the will of the
collectivity. In reality this type of legal
system conceals an order of labor, of power, and
of goods no less purposeful than that of feudalism according to Renner. Thus his analysis of the
social function of law and its transformation
under capitalism is central to his sociology of
law.[40]

The main concern of Renner's sociology of
law is the change in the function of the property
concept in a dynamic society. He adopts the positivist legal theory of ownership which states
that the normal beneficial use of tangible things
is legally irrelevant. What an owner does with
his property is not the concern of the law. The
latter is only concerned when another withholds
possession, or disturbs the owner's enjoyment of
his property, or when one acquires or loses his
right of ownership. A differentiation between
the legal and sociological concepts of property
is made by Renner. He follows Roman law in
dealing with the ownership concept which considers ownership as a relation between an individual and his property rights. Property is
defined as a right in an individual tangible
object only (i.e., land or a movable thing).[41]

The analysis of the functional transformation of legal institutions in western society
according to Renner takes as a starting point the
time when the bulk of all goods producers were
independent peasants and artisans who owned their
means of production, employed little outside
labor, and sold their products directly to the
consumer (i.e., circa 1600 AD). The law of
property was paramount with only the contract of
work and labor having importance. Renner compares
this social order with that existing in 1900
stating that the law of property is approximately
the same but its social functions have changed.
Property law coupled with contract law adapted to
new social objectives where both blue and white
collar workers were becoming part of a new order
of labor and power whereby the corporation becomes the owner of property and controls all who
work within the corporate structure, and also
manipulates the law of the state to its own
ends.[42]

The law has very little to do with the
formation and operation of groups whether corporate or municipal according to Renner. He
states that nothing is law except the control of
people by other people regardless of the type of
social forces keeping the group together (i.e.,
public versus private corporation).

Renner points out that by 1900 the ownership
of tangible things became property in industrial
capital and this in turn transformed other legal
institutions.[43] For example he points out the
destruction of the economic base of family law
and in its place the rise of the welfare state;
the decline in importance of the law of inheritance; the contract of sale becomes subservient
to the law of property creating changes in the
law of sale; and changes in the contracts of loan,
sale, employment, and lease. Last, Renner shows

that the modern loan, joint stock company, lease
mortgage, and other related legal institutions
brought about freedom for capital which enabled
it to alter basic societal legal structures and
their norms by 1900. He uses the evolution of
the law of property as it affects the family as
his model (i.e., from 1600 to 1900 AD).[44]

Kahn-Freund points out that Renner's positivist doctrine belongs to the age of liberal
capitalism, where the latter could study the
functioning of the "property norm" in isolation
from public law. In contemporary society, public
law in part determines and alters the economic
and social functions of property. Renner cor-
rectly shows that legal institutions may thor-
oughly change their social function as a consequence of a transformation in their environment
according to Kahn-Freund. These changes not only
show how the function of the legal norm is transformed by developments of the economy but also
how the courts adapt the content of the norm to
its function.[45]

Sawer in his essay, "Law As Socially Neutral:
Karl Renner" indicates that Renner emphasizes the
adaptability of legal institutions. In particular,
he deals with the larger social transitions particularly from the last stages of feudalism to the
early stages of modern capitalism. His main theme
stresses the way in which the socalled property
norm is adapted to serve the complex purposes of
Western capitalist society.[46]

The main propositions of Renner are: (1)
fundamental changes in society are possible without accompanying alterations of the legal system;
(2) the law does not cause economic development;
(3) economic change does not immediately and
automatically bring about change in the law; and
(4) the social sub-stratum develops slowly by

evolution, not by revolution. Renner also lists
four of the ways in which legal norms adapt to
social change.[47]

Legal institutions are of concern to Renner.
He defines them as property, contract, marriage,
family, heirship, insolvency, corporate personality, etc. He also defines legal institution as
a governing legal relationship regulating a basic
circumstance of life. Further he defines the
basic circumstances of life as a part of the
social sub-stratum of law possessing the character of a social unit, a set of social relationships. Renner's concept of legal institution is
rather indeterminate according to Sawer. There
are important differences between the kinds of
legal rules which make up some institutions as
compared with others. Renner demonstrates that
adaptability is inherent in certain kinds of
legal rules. He is also concerned with legal
values and institutions that survive from one
social order to another despite fundamental
economic changes. Finally he wants to show that
these holdover institutions do not prevent change
as society evolves but could be used and altered
for new socio-legal purposes without losing their
formal identity.[48]

The concern of Renner with the property norm
(his main thesis) is taken from his Marxian view
of the sociology and legal history of the transition to capitalism. He uses the evolution of the
institution of property in Western society as an
illustration of his central thesis. He also
develops corollaries to his main thesis which to
Sawer are more important than his discourse on the
property norm (i.e., the evolution of the traditional contract of labor to the modern contract of
labor; and the development of the concepts of
legal character mask and complementary legal
institution).[49]

The study of the relations between his concepts of legal institution and social institution
is Renner's contribution to the sociology of law
according to Sawer. This relation demonstrates
the tendency of a society to associate a particular set of legal norms with a particular social
institution or purpose, even though the legal
norms are formally stated in a way which does not
make this connection clear (i.e., the attempt to
explain popular uses of the expression "legal
fiction" or the term "legalistic" as compared
with the term "legal").[50]

Huntington Cairns

Cairns in his book, Law and the Social
Sciences reviews the contributions that sociology
has made to the field of law. He states that the
contributions are along the lines of (1) sociological theories of the nature of law, (2) sociological method in law, (3) sociological analysis
of socio-legal institutions, and (4) social
change and legal change.[51]

He reviews the sociological theories of the
nature of law of Montesquieu, Comte, Spencer,
Ward, Ross, and MacIver. Cairns feels that
Montesquieu who defined law as the necessary
relations arising from the nature of things was
the first concerned with the sociological approach
to law. Comte held no definite sociological
theory of law while Spencer set forth a theory of
the origin of law. Law to the latter was an
embodiment of ancestral injunctions. Ward regarded law as a derivative institution and merely
a sentiment.[52]

The sociological theory of law is divided
into two groups by Cairns. These are theorists
who accept the theory of law held by lawyers and

theorists whose theories of law are equated with
the term social control. The former group are
considered the followers of Pound and are not
dealt with to any extent by Cairns. The latter
group are typified by Ross and MacIver. Ross was
the first sociologist to write of law as a method
of social control while MacIver's sociology of
law attempted to differentiate clearly between
custom and law. The latter defines law as the
body of rules which are recognized, interpreted,
and applied to particular situations by the
courts of the state.[53]

A number of jurists such as Holmes, Cardozo,
and Maitland use the sociological approach or
method in jurisprudence according to Cairns. He
mentions a number of areas where sociological
analysis of socio-legal institutions has taken
place, such as institutional studies and crime/
criminal behavior studies. Last, Cairns reviews
the work of Ogburn on social change and legal
change. This analysis is based on Ogburn's
theory of socio-cultural change.[54]

Roscoe Pound

To Pound in his essay, "Sociology of Law"
the term's meaning depends in part upon the definition of the legal concept. He lists six broad
areas in which the concept of law has been defined
by Roman and Anglo-American jurisprudents. Law
is defined by Pound as a system of authoritative
materials for grounding or guiding judicial and
administrative action recognized or established in
a politically organized society while a law is the
equivalent of loi. He also defines law sociologically as social control through the systematic application of the force of politically organized
society. Therefore the sociology of law is sociology applied to the study of the legal order (i.e.

of the body of authoritative grounds of or guides
to decision in accordance with which that regime
is maintained by the judicial and administrative
process). Finally Pound categorizes law into
three processes: the legal order, the authoritative grounds of or guides to determination of
disputes in societies, and the judicial and administrative processes.[55]

There must be a convergence of the sociological and juristic approaches to have a field
of sociology of law according to Pound. He examines both the sociological and juristic approaches in order to provide background for understanding the sociology of law. The first theorist
picked by Pound was Montesquieu who saw law as an
integral part of social life which serves as a
control agent. Comte had only vague ideas of law.
Spencer considered law as political institutions
put together by a politically organized society.
Durkheim explained law as the expression of a
basic social fact and distinguished repressive law
from restitutive law. Ross hypothesized that law
is a form of social control. Weber dealt with law
as a value system concerned with claims and demands and developed a theory of interests. To
Ehrlich law meant social control, consisted of a
body of social norms, and created the concept of
the living law. Timasheff's sociology of law was
theoretical and considered law to be a right.
Gurvitch considered law as generalized social
control but in a social philosophical sense.[56]

The juristic line of approach begins with the
theoretical works of Savigny and Maine. By the
end of the 19th century, three juristic movements
develop; the Marxian view; the philosophy of law
view of Jhering, Stammler, and Kohler; and the
sociological typified by the writings of Duguit,
Hauriou, and Pound himself. The latter states
that sociological jurisprudence began with an

ethnological interpretation of law; moved towards
a psychological orientation based on the works of
Von Gierke, Ward, and Tarde; and has evolved from
the sociological influences of Ross, Weber, and
Ehrlich (i.e., concepts of social control and
interests). He lists Holmes, Cardozo, and
Llewellyn as contemporary adherents to modern
sociological jurisprudence.[57]

Nicholus S. Timasheff

Timasheff in his book, An Introduction to the
Sociology of Law is a nomographic science which
aims at discovering rules of a scientific nature
concerning society in its relation to law. The
object of sociology of law is the determination
and consideration of human behavior in society
by the existence of legal norms using the causal-
functional approach. Timasheff defines law as a
specific social force or of socially imposed rules
acting on human behavior. Thus law is a form of
social coordination (i.e., is closely connected
to social equilibrium and to basic social
phenomena). Law's social function is imposing
norms of conduct or patterns of social behavior on
the individual will.[58]

The sociological study of law cannot be an
adjunct to the study of jurisprudence (i.e., legal
norms) since it is impossible to construct a
system of knowledge which accurately combine the
formal study of norms with the causal study of
human behavior related to these norms. Timasheff
states three propositions concerning the correlation between the sociology of law and jurisprudence. These are (1) sociology of law content
depends only slightly on changes in legal regulations; (2) there is only one sociology of law
while many jurisprudences exist; and (3) sociology
of law is a nomographic science.[59]

Timasheff deals with the relationship of
legal sociology and philosophy of law to a great
extent, attempts to show the relationship between
sociology of law and psychology, points out what
methodology should be utilized by sociology of law,
and enumerates topics that the field of legal
sociology should investigate.[60]

In an essay, "Growth and Scope of Sociology
of Law" Timasheff gives a detailed review of the
evolution of the field since World War I as he
surveys legal sociology in an attempt to find
answers to how law and society are related. He
classes the research on this topice into six
areas: (1) American neo-realism, (2) Max Weber
and legitimate order analysis, (3) Russian
sociology and the distinction between the legal
and moral order, (4) the Upsala school, (5) legal
philosophers, and (6) cultural anthropology.[61]

The American neo-realists characterized by the
writings of Frank and Llewellyn have created no
tangible body of knowledge dealing with the sociology of law. Weber attempts to formulate a general theory of the two basic types of legal
activity (i.e., law creating and law finding or
adjudication). The Russian school consists of the
students of Petrazhitsky who made the distinction
between the legal and moral orders. These followers were Sorokin, Gurvitch, and Timasheff. Members
of the Upsala school share the idea that a theory
of law demands the elimination of the idealism of
law as a fact and as a system of normative ideas.
This school consists of Hagerstrom, Olivecrona,
Ross, and Geiger. Timasheff mentions a number of
legal philosophers whose theories attempt to inte-
grate law with society such as Kelsen, Horvath,
Schindler, Haesaert, Coing, Pound, Cairns, and
Hall. Lastly such anthropologists as Malinowski,
Linton, Hoebel, and Hall are mentioned along with
their contributions to sociology of law.[62]

Georges Gurvitch

Gurvitch in his book, Sociology of Law deals
in great detail with the forerunners and founders
of legal sociology. The forerunners are divided
into Aristotle, Hobbes, Spinoza, and Montesquieu.
These are followed by Grotius, Leibnitz, Fitchte,
Savigny, Puchta, Saint-Simon, and Gierke. The
later forerunners are categorized as legal his-
torians, comparative law specialists, jural eth-
nologists, and criminologists. The last group
consists of Maine, de Coulanges, Ihering, Post,
Frazer, Lombroso, Ferry, and Tarde. Gurvitch
divided the founders into European and American
categories. The former consist of Durkheim,
Duguit, Hauriou, Weber, and Ehrlich while the
latter founders consist of Holmes, Pound, Cardozo,
Llewellyn, and Arnold.[63]

The sociology of law according to Gurvitch
studies the full social reality of law in all its
dimentional levels. He divides legal sociology
into three parts because society is composed of a
multiplicity of particular groups, each group in
turn being composed of a multiplicity of ways of
being linked to the whole by the whole. Thus the
law framework corresponds to the types of legal
groups (i.e., union law, state law, canon law) and
also corresponds to systems of law which correspond
to types of inclusive societies (i.e., feudal law,
European law, primitive law).[64]

A hierarchy of problems is imposed on the
sociology of law according to Gurvitch. Without
the systematic sociology of law there is no genetic
sociology of law. The systematic or microsociology
of law is the study of the manifestations of law as
a function of the form of sociality and of the
levels of social reality. The differential sociology of law is the study of law as a function of
real collective units whose solution is found in
the juridical typology of particular groups and inclusive societies. The genetic or macrosociology

of law is the study of regularities as tendencies
and factors of the development, change and decay
of the law within a particular type of society.[65]

The microsociology of law consists of what
Gurvitch calls social law, interpersonal law, and
intergroup law. Law is defined as a relationship
between claims and duties made to correspond with
each other by a social guarantee of normative
facts. There exists three types of interpersonal
law: (1) of separation, (2) of rapproachment, and
(3) mixed law. Law consists of a series of gradu-
ated levels which fit into two mutually exclusive
classifications. The first consists of organized
law and below it unorganized law. The second consists of fixed law, flexible law, and intuitive
law. Lastly Gurvitch states that every type of
law consists of six levels. These are (1) fixed
organized law, (2) flexible organized law, (3)
organized intuitive law, (4) fixed spontaneous law,
(5) flexible spontaneous law, and (6) intuitive
spontaneous law.[66]

Differential sociology of law includes within
its realm Gurvitch's classification of the juridical typology of particular groupings. The groupings are classified according to scope, duration,
function, attitude, ruling organizational principle, form of constraint, and degree of unity within
an organized superstructure. The conclusion of the
juridical typology of groups allows one to establish types of legal systems found in societies.
Gurvitch states there are seven types of societies
each with its own legal system. These are: (1)
polysegmentary, (2) homogeneous having theocratic-
charismatic basis, (3) homogeneous having domestic-
political basis, (4) feudal, (5) city-empire, (6)
territorial state, and (7) contemporary.[67]

The macrosociology of law is concerned with
the transformation of law. Gurvitch rejects the

social evolutionary treatises of Maine, Durkheim, and Sumner concerning the evolution of law in society. He states that it is quite difficult to trace legal institution changes in one type of society let alone in two types of society since one must consider the relation of the legal institution to all other institutions which may be effected differentially by changes in the legal structure or by judicial decisions.[68]

William M. Evan

In the introduction to his reader, Law and Sociology, Evan states there are five distinct approaches to the sociology of law. Underlying these approaches are the comparative and historical dimensions of analysis. The role analysis approach focuses on legal statuses and concerns recruitment practices, professional socialization, colleague relationships, etc. The second approach or organizational analysis deals with the nature of the organizational structure of courts, administrative agencies, and enforcement agencies. The normative analysis approach deals with legal norms in relation to their underlying values and to the social units or status groupings that are the object of legal norms. The fourth approach or institutional analysis concerns itself with legitimation and interpretation of rules, applications of sanctions, and determinations of jurisdiction. The methodological approach uses sociological research techniques that can be applied to legal institution analysis.[69]

F. James Davis

Davis in an essay, "The Sociological Study of Law" reviews the growth and development of the sociology of law. He starts his review by

examining early 20th century jurisprudence to show
some of the problems as well as areas of cooperation between sociology and jurisprudence. Pound
and Llewellyn as jurisprudents argue for such
cooperation along with Riesman and Rose from the
sociological perspective.[70]

Sociological jurisprudence, legal realism, the
philosophy of law, and comparative law are examined by Davis. He reviews the work of Holmes,
Pound, Cardozo, Llewellyn, Frank, Arnold, Maine,
Wigmore, and the work of Simpson and Stone. The
part played by the concept of social control upon
sociology of law in the United States is analyzed
by Davis through writings of such theorists as
Ross, Cooley, Landis, Bernard, Roucek, and LaPiere.
This orientation is compared with the role of
European sociology of law in the founding of the
field. Durkheim, Ehrlich, Timasheff, Gurvitch,
and Weber are dealt with in terms of their definitions of law and their statements about the functions and structure of the field.[71]

The definition of law is analyzed from the
European writers' perspective as a system of
values recognized and declared by political officials by Davis. This tradition defined justice as
the condition of reasonably satisfactory equilibrium. European theorists were oriented toward
dealing with law in terms of "what is right"
while American theorists view law as "political
force". Most American theorists have used Pound's
definition of law (i.e., law as social control
through the systematic application of the force
of politically organized society).[72]

Sociology's contribution to sociology of law
should be its theory of social control and should
serve as a tool to reform the legal institution.
Documentary research (i.e., historical) should be
its method of research.[73]

In an essay, "Law As A Type of Social Control",
Davis defines social control as the process by
which subgroups and persons are influenced to conduct themselves in conformity to group expectations.
Social control may be exerted consciously or uncon-
sciously by means of positive and negative sanctions.
These sanctions can be formal or informal, sugges-
tive, persuasive, or coercive. Social control
facilitates social order and group unity as it is
related to the concept of socialization.[74]

Law is defined by Davis as the formal means of
social control that involves the use of rules that
are interpreted, and are enforceable, by the courts
of a political community. His definition of law is
consistent with that of Pound and MacIver although
the latter limits his definition to legal rules.
Davis' definition is restricted to the political
community although it is neither intended to support the idea that the expressed will of the state
is absolutely sovereign nor is it intended to pre-
clude the use of materials about preliterate or
other systems of social control that do not have
courts or other requisites of law as defined.[75]

Law should be viewed as an approximation to
the ideal type of formal social control although it
may be expected to be closely related to certain
informal controls such as shaming and ostracism to
name a few. Legal rules specify proper conduct for
the citizen, are directed toward legal officials,
and serve as conduct guides for rule enforcement
officials. Thus legal rules clarify role rights
and duties and also provide sanctions to support
them. Law as a formal social control agency makes
provisions for designated persons to play specialized roles. Unless there are official agencies and
specialists (i.e., courts and judges) to decide
disputes by interpreting and applying legal rules
to given situations, there is no law as defined
by Davis.[76]

Law is a means of control employed by a
political community (i.e., the state) that involves forcible maintenance of orderly domination
over a territory and its inhabitants. The state
is not absolutely sovereign due to the fact that
people have the power to resist, because of constitutional safeguards preventing governmental
monopoly of power, due to lack of knowledge of all
statutes by the populace, and because many parties
to a dispute fail to initiate legal action.[77]

Davis states that the definitions of law in
European legal sociology have been related to the
rejection of the concept of absolute state sovereignty. These theorists state that law and
courts existed prior to the political community
and do not depend on it. A better view is that
government is but one phase of formal social control in society, and as social organization
becomes less Gemeinschaft with informal controls
become inadequate, political institutions emerge
to meet the needs of a Gesellschaft society.[78]

The kinds of law are dealt with by classi-
fying law from three viewpoints. These are: (1)
content, (2) origin, and (3) degree of rationality
in the legal system. Davis classes law content as
substantive and procedural (sometimes called
adjective or remedial), distinguishes public from
private law, and differentiates criminal law from
civil law.[79]

Law is sometimes classified on the basis of
its origin. The distinction is between legislation
and case law. Legislation is divided into consti-
tutions, treaties, statutes, ordinances, administrative regulations, and court rules. Statutes
are classified as to whether they are enabling,
remedial, or penal. Case law or judge-made law is
synonymous with the common law while enacted law
is synonymous with legislation. The distinction

between the common law, civil law, and equity law is also made by Davis.[80]

Weber's classification of legal systems on the degree of rationality is important according to Davis. He states the reference is to the type of legal thought involved in the administration of justice. Weber distinguishes between formal rationality and substantive rationality. He identifies three types of administration of justice: Khadi justice (i.e., religion-based), empirical justice (i.e., Anglo-American system), and rational justice (i.e., Roman Empire law).[81]

Davis examines law as a part of culture by perceiving law as a set of social institutions and as an index of values and social solidarity. He also looks at law and ethics and legal specialists to gain more about law's place in the cultural context. Law is an institutional part of the culture and cannot exist independently of other societal institutions since all legal acts concern and are instrumental in making choices and in organizing institutional value systems. The limits within which legal controls operate are determined by the values supported by other social institutions. Thus legal and law enforcement decisions will be uncertain and equivocal where there is ambivalence or disagreement as to values priority.[82]

Law helps in the process of value integration. Some sociologists maintain that law is so intimately connected with other societal institutions that it can serve as an index of societal values. Law can serve as an indicator of political stability and also serve as a measure of the type of societal unity or solidarity (i.e., Ehrlich's idea of law as a mirror of group norms and Durkheim's typology, homogeneous society=repressive law while heterogeneous society=restitutive law).[83]

Sociology of law theorists agree with the exception of Timasheff that law and ethics are different. If acts that are considered immoral do not directly harm other people, the law may ignore them but the law may proscribe acts that threaten society even though they are not considered immoral. The law should not be strictly separated from those moral rules that are generally accepted in the political community. Some of the law reflects the adoption of particular moral precepts and the concern for justice.[84]

Talcott Parsons

Parsons in an essay, "The Law and Social Control" states that law concerns patterns, norms, and rules that are applied to the acts and roles of persons and to the collectivities of which they are members. Law deals with normative patterns to which various kinds of sanctions are applied. Any social relationship can be regulated by law. Law can be considered a generalized mechanism of social control that operates diffusely in all sections of society. Parsons defines law as a set of rules backed by certain types of sanctions, legitimized in certain ways, and applied in certain ways. Law as a mechanism of social control is partly a function of societal social equilibrium since acute societal value conflict or serious enforcement problems cause law to be ineffectual.[85]

He mentions four basic problems of the legal system: (1) the basis of legitimation of the system of rules, (2) interpretation (i.e., the meaning of the rule for two persons in a particular situation in particular roles), (3) sanctions (i.e., the favorable or unfavorable consequences that should follow from conforming or not conforming to the rules), and (4) jurisdiction (i.e., to whom

and under what circumstances a rule or rule complex with its interpretations and sanctions
applies).[86]

The primary function of a legal system is
integrative since it serves to mitigate potential
elements of conflict and maintains social intercourse. The second function in law is the legit-
imative which concerns the relation and distinction
between law and ethics. The legal system must
always rest on proper legitimation which may take
forms rather close to the legal process itself
(i.e., enactment by proper procedures by duly
authorized bodies). The third function in law is
the interpretive which has two aspects, rule-
focused (i.e., the integrity of the systems of
rules itself) and client-focused (i.e., relation of
rules to the individuals, groups, and collectivities
on whom they impinge). The interpretive function
is the central function of a legal system according
to Parsons. Performance of the latter function is
facilitated by structural devices such as judicial
independence from political pressure, professional-
ization of the judicial role, and institutionaliza-[87]
tion of the decision-making process.

Normative consistency is one of the most important criteria of effectiveness of a legal system
(i.e., rules formulated in the system must not
subject individuals under its jurisdiction to in-
compatible expectations or obligations). The assum-
ing of responsibility for functions where there are
no clearly correct answers can be ascertained as a
source of strain for the legal profession. Various
types of legal deviance can occur in reaction to
these strains such as (1) yielding to expediency
through financial and other pressures, (2) exaggerated legal formalism (i.e., following the letter
of the law without regard for the reality of the
situation), and (3) yielding to the exaggerated

claims of clients or other interests represented
by lawyers.[88]

The legal profession stands between public
authority and its norms and the client (individual
or group) whose conduct or intentions may not be
in accord with the law. The profession functions
ideally to socialize the client about the legal
institution and to forestall deviance on the
client's part. The effective performance of these
functions depends on whether their role performance
meets certain conditions such as the confidential
nature of lawyer-client.[89]

Vilhelm Aubert

Aubert in an article, "Researches In the
Sociology of Law" defines law as a regularity of
behavior, primarily an invariance in judicial
decision-making. The sociology of law deals with
the relationship between theoretical and social
structures. Law has two functions: to create
conformity with norms, and to settle conflicts.
The structure of legal thinking is functionally
determined by the social situations in which the
tasks are carried out.[90]

The primary task of sociology of law is to
relate the structure of legal thinking to the
recurrent types of social interactions on which
it is brought to bear. Aubert feels that a
sociological analysis of law cannot be separated
from a philosophical analysis of law or from
jurisprudence. He lists six characteristics of
legal thinking that sets it apart from the kind of
thinking that applies to the social sciences.[91]

Jerome Skolnick

Skolnick in his article, "The Sociology of
Law In America: Overview and Trends" characterizes
the development of sociology of law through three
fundamental conflicts: (1) American society projects an egalitarian value system but displays to
all a caste-like stratification structure: (2)
although paying lip service to the Gemeinschaft
myth of local control and direct participation in
government, America is Gesellschaft in orientation
and purpose; and (3) the economic power of society
rests with an elite that controls society despite
the belief that power belongs to the people.
American sociology of law has addressed itself to
these apparent social contradictions according to
Skolnick.[92]

Sociology of law studies in America has not
been related to each other or to an overriding
theoretical concern. Skolnick summarizes the
studies utilizing a conflict theme and characterizes the fundamental concerns generated by the
intellectual environment which have influenced the
kinds of topics selected by sociologists of law.
Due to the complexity of the literature on anthropology of law and sociological jurisprudence, he
only superficially deals with these two essential
areas pertaining to law in society.[93]

Virtually all empirical sociology of law
studies in America began after 1950 according to
Skolnick. He begins by tracing the roots of
American sociology of law to the field of juris-
prudence and the writing of Holmes, Pound, Brandeis,
Llewellyn, and Frank.

The relationship between social stratification and the administration of justice is examined
by an analysis of the Chicago Jury Study, the
legal profession, and poverty studies. Skolnick

concludes that these studies add little to the
theoretical knowledge of the sociology of law.
Justice in mass society is examined by an analysis
of studies dealing with law and morality, social
science and legal needs, and jurimetrics.
Skolnick deals with the shift in the law from an
adjudicative to an administrative character using
Tappan's delinquency study as an example. Another
issue concerning the mass administration of justice
is the relation between law and conventional morality. He hypothesizes that the wider the range of
prohibited conduct, the less likely that law can be
administered fairly. Skolnick concludes that the
field of criminology has many studies bearing some
relation to sociology of law and are potential
areas for sociology of law research.[94]

Skolnick feels the most important work for the
sociologist of law is the development of theory
growing out of empirical institutional studies. It
is easier to develop a model for the criminal
court than for the civil court. Research on jurimetrics and judicial decision-making are also of
use to sociology of law. The field should also be
concerned with justice and private (i.e., corporate)
government. Skolnick reviews the concepts of
legality and legal systems, legal control, and
social control in bureaucratic settings. Selznick's
view of legality is utilized by Skolnick to suggest
that the sociology of law should be concerned with
the existence of legal orders in different social
settings (i.e., corporate bodies).[95]

There is a tendency toward legality as an
inherent characteristic of human society (i.e., as
man obtains more freedom he may need more law).
Further the function of law and the procedures of
adjudication bear an essential similarity in nonliterate societies to the functions and forms of
law in Western society. Law could also be viewed

as the purposive enterprise of subjecting human
conduct to the governance of rules. These views
are expressed by Selznick, Llewellyn, and Hoebel.[96]

Skolnick concludes with an analysis of sociology of law and social theory. He feels that
sociological research in America is comparative,
jurisprudential, and reflective of contemporary
sociological trends. The trend in research is the
analysis of legal development and legal change
using historical trends (i.e., what social conditions produce various substantive and procedural
phenomena in the legal realm). The most general
contribution that sociology of law can make to
social theory is that of understanding the relation
between law and social organization. Not all rules
are lawful rules, and sociologists ignore the rule
of law in society. Thus there is a confusion of
legalism with legality, of rules of law with a rule
of law. Sociology of law should be concerned with
the legal conditions and consequences of the social
order. It is interested in the nature of legality
and in the conditions under which it is most likely
to emerge. Lastly the field should require a
categorization of legality which takes both the
ideal and the procedural for obtaining it into
account as this categorization would enable the
study of conditions under which different types of
legality tend to emerge.[97]

Geoffrey Sawer

Sawer in his book, Law In Society states that
there cannot be a sociology of law as a whole at
least in relation to complex modern societies. A
successful paradigm of law in society does not and
will not exist. This does not mean that there is
no such thing as a sociology of law since general
propositions dealing with law can be formulated
with regard to particular legal situations or with

social relations associated with a particular type
of legal rule. Sawer believes there is no sociology of law in the sense of a body of learning
peculiar to social situations in which legal rules
or the behavior of persons in response to legal
rules are prominent or are the main focus of
interest. There is a sharp distinction between
the sociology of law and sociological jurisprudence but it is more ideal than real.[98]

The sociological view of the legal institution
depends on an apparatus of state administration
while the anthropological view depends on societal
forces or functional relations. Primitive law can
be differentiated from the modern law and examined
without reference to the latter. We can see in
primitive societies what may be the origins of
legal systems but the importance of such studies
is to show that relatively complex social arrange-
ments can be maintained for long periods without
the institutions which in modern society are regarded as necessary for "rule of law". The
material content of a legal system reflects the
needs or demands of society.[99]

Various attempts have been made to classify
social relations of law such as Kohler's theory of
jural postulates, Ihering's theory of social interests, or Pound's use of both theories. Pound
identifies four basic jural postulates applicable
to American society. Hoebel also uses the concept
of jural postulates in order to explain the legally
relevant social features of traditional cultures.
His statements are social claims or attitudes which
could be expected to affect legal development
whereas Pound's statements are a mixture of such
social claims of the legal formulations into which
they are translated.[100]

The interests approach goes into greater
detail than the theory of postulates. Law is

conceived as a method of giving effect to interests.
Law's task is to classify these interests on the
basis of some value system so as to determine which
interests are to be given effect and which to be
rejected. Interests exist independent of the law.
An interest is defined as a claim actually advanced
by "defined" individuals or groups and considered
and dealt with by "defined" lawmakers and courts.
This is a good way of stating the relation between
law and society according to Sawer.[101]

Philip Selznick

Selznick in his article, "The Sociology of Law"
states there are three basic stages in the development of the sociology of law. The primitive stage
of communicating a perspective has been accomplished
through the theoretical work of European social
scientists coupled with the sociological perspective
of American legal scholars who have been influenced
by European theory. The second stage is that of
sociological craftsmanship. This is where law areas
are explored in depth, problems are analyzed, and
sociological techniques and ideas are brought to
bear on the legal institution. Selznick believes
that sociology of law is in the second stage of
development. The third stage is concerned with
theory building and is where theories of law can be
formulated.[102]

Law is defined by Selznick as a social phenomenon, an important agency of social control. There
is an implicit recognition that not all law is on
the same level, as some law is inferior because it
contains a wrong mixture of arbitrary sovereign
will, including majority will, judge-made law, and
legislative law. Legality is based on a combination
of sovereign will and objective reason. Sociology
of law needs to develop both a broad theoretical
perspective and an emphasis on societal needs and
institutional potentialities. Any effort to ground

legal doctrine on sociological theory must be
based on theories of the origin of the American
social order and the direction in which society is
evolving. Such developmental models are the most
likely to have something significant to say about
the probable evolution of the law.[103]

In an essay entitled, "The Sociology of Law"
written for the International Encyclopedia of the
Social Sciences, Selznick states that the aim of
sociology of law is the extension of knowledge regarding the foundations of a legal order, the pattern of legal change, and law's contribution to the
fulfillment of social needs and aspirations. The
sociology of law realm overlaps with criminology
and political sociology in its area of inquiry.[104]

The roots of sociology of law lie mainly in
jurisprudence rather than in sociology. Selznick
refers to such theorists as Ehrlich and Pound who
were influenced by such social theorists as Weber,
Durkheim, Ross and Sumner. Four basic motifs have
been prominant in the history of sociology of law
(i.e., historicism, instrumentalism, antiformalism,
and pluralism) according to Selznick. Historicism
traces legal ideas and institutions to their historical roots and is exemplified by the work of
Maine, Holmes, Weber, and Durkheim. Instrumentalism calls for the assessment of law according to
defined social purposes and invites close study of
what law is and does in fact (exemplified by the
writings of Bentham and Pound). Antiformalism
emphasizes the purity of law as a formal isolated
system, is concerned with abstract and general
concepts of legal rules, and is exemplified by the
writing of Ehrlich and American legal realists.
Pluralism is the sociological approach, refers to
the view that law is located in society, and is
also found in the writings of Ehrlich.[105]

Selznick discusses Weber's definition of law stating that it allows for extra-state law (i.e., ecclesiastical law and corporate law) as well as law of the political community. Thus Weber's approach to law takes into consideration all types of law but does not offer a satisfactory theory for identifying the requirements of a legal order. An adequate theory of law must identify the distinctive work done by law in society, the special resources of law, and the characteristic mechanisms that law brings into play.[106]

The key word in any discussion of law is authority, not coercion according to Selznick as legality presumes the emergence of authoritative norms whose status is guaranteed by evidence of other consensually validated rules. The special work of law is to identify claims and obligations that merit official validation or enforcements. Thus when institutions emerge that do this work, we can speak of a legal order. An authoritative act asserts a claim to obedience, and the reach of that claim determines whether and to what extent a legal system exists. Weber saw the relation of the legal and the authoritative. Coercion does not make law though it may establish an order out of which law may emerge. Authority, consensus, and rationality have a definite place in any definition of law according to Selznick.[107]

Law aims at a moral achievement, namely legality or the rule of law. The study of legality is the chief preoccupation of sociology of law in Selznick's scheme of things. The main task of sociology of law is the discovery of which social conditions are congenial to the rule of law and which undermine it. Selznick presents four topics which provide a framework in which research on legality can be pursued: (1) transition from legitimacy to legality, (2) rational consensus and civic competence, (3) institutionalized criticism, and (4) institutionalized self-restraint. The transition from legitimacy to legality requires the recognition that official acts can be questioned and appraised. The consensus that sustains legality entails deepened public understanding of the complex meaning of freedom under law. If the ideals of legality are to be fulfilled, institutional criticism must be built into the machinery of lawmaking and administration. The legal system depends heavily on self-restraint and thus on social mechanisms for building in appropriate values and rules of conduct.[108]

The conditions that strengthen or weaken the rule of law can be examined by historically placing the evolution of legality in a social change context and relating law to the development of other social institutions including culturally defined conceptions of authority and justice. The extension of legality to new institutions and settings occurs mainly within government although there has been a movement toward legal restraint of arbitrary decision making in nongovernmental institutions in Western society. There is a conflict between administration and legality since procedural safeguards are costly in time, energy, and ability to deal equitably with all.[109]

Incipient law refers to a compelling claim of right or a practice so viable and important to a functioning institution as to make legal recognition probable in due course. Incipient legal change bridges the concepts of law and social order as it assumes that law has a distinctive nature. Some law is seen as latent in the evolving social and economic order.[110]

Law is an active agent of social change, and research should center about its function as a change agent and the problems associated with legal change. Legislation, administration, and common

law are significant for social change, with legislation the most obvious way of effecting social
change through law. The most basic resource of
the law for social change is the set of legal
principles that can be invoked to justify action
in their name.[111]

Large scale social changes in society have
contributed to a vast increase in the tasks that
must be assumed by the contemporary legal order.
The first trend has been the shift from Gemeinschaft to Gesellschaft social order that has
greatly increased pressure on formal agencies of
service and regulation. The second trend has been
the emergence of the large corporate organizations
as the representative societal institution and
problems it has caused the law. Third has been the
ascendance of social interests over parochial
interests.[112]

Much current research centers on social
aspects of the administration of justice. Moral
significance of the law studies have emphasized
law's role in creating deviance. Other research
includes studies of public opinion and the law.
The major problem of sociology of law remains the
integration of jurisprudence research and sociological research. Unless this integration is
accomplished, sociology of law will be of peripheral importance to both sociology and law in
general.[113]

Paul Bohannon

In an essay entitled, "Law and Legal Institutions" written for the International Encyclopedia
of the Social Sciences, Bohannon states that laws
are not social acts but precepts in terms of which
people are supposed to act. There must be a
social act which people regard as a wrong way to

behave which will undermine societal institutions
for a legal situation to exist. Once a person
oversteps the accepted permissible range of
deviation, a counteraction takes place so that the
breach of standards can be corrected. Bohannon
deals primarily with examples of the criminal law
to illustrate his theoretical points.[114]

There are many kinds of what Bohannon calls
counteracting institutions in society such as
courts, lawyers, and police systems. Self-help is
a universal counteracting institution since within
defined limits a wronged person has societal
permission to bring about the correction of the
situation by which he was wronged. The game solution which defines for people the range of rules
whereby life is largely played is another type of
counteracting institution, while the town-meeting
also serves as a form of counteraction.[115]

A successful counteraction is followed by a
series of acts called the correction by Bohannon.
Deviant acts can be corrected by making the person
who committed the original wrong carry out the
action in terms of the norm being violated or by
implying some sort of penalty.[116]

Bohannon shows through an analysis of several
studies how difficult it is to delimit the subject
matter of law. He quotes from the writings of such
theorists as Hart, Stone, Pospisil, and Kantorowicz
to illustrate the characteristics and attributes of
law in order to better understand the concept of
legality.[117]

Law must be distinguished from traditions and
fashions. More specifically it must be differentiated from social norm and from custom according
to Bohannon. Law is specifically recreated by
agents of society in a narrower and recognizable
context than custom. Law includes custom but it

must also consist of rules capable of reinterpretation by one of society's legal institutions so
that the conflicts within nonlegal institutions
can be adjusted by legal authority. A distinction
can be made between law and custom. Reciprocity
is the basis of custom. All institutions including
the legal one develop customs. Some customs are
restated (i.e., reinstitutionalized) for the more
precise purposes of legal institutions. A custom
that has been restated in order to make it amenable
to the activities of the legal institutions is
therefore law. Law is never a reflection of
custom.[118]

A legal institution in society allows people
to settle their disputes and also it counteracts
any abuses of the rules of other societal institutions. Legal institutions face the tasks of (1)
disengaging institutions from difficulties and
engaging the difficulties within the legal institutional processes; (2) handling trouble-cases
within the legal institutional framework; and (3)
reengaging trouble-case solutions within the
processes of the institution where all the trouble
began. There are two aspects of legal institutions
that are not shared with other societal institutions. These are the regularized ways of interference in the dysfunctioning non-legal institutions in order to disengage the trouble-case; and
the types of rules utilized by the legal institutions (i.e., procedural and substantive).[119]

Law is defined by Bohannon as a body of binding obligations regarded as right by one party and
acknowledged as a duty by the other which has been
reinstitutionalized within the legal institution
so that society can continue to function in an
orderly manner on the basis of rules so maintained.[120]

Legal rights are those rights that attach to
norms that have been reinstitutionalized. Thus a
legal right is the restatement of some but never
all of the recognized claims of the persons within
societal institutions made for the purpose of
maintaining peaceful and just operations of societal institutions.[121]

Edwin M. Schur

Schur in his book, Law and Society: A
Sociological View states that the legal system is
important as a major institutional complex within
society. A Society's legal system is embedded in
and generates a distinctive and coherent though
changing set of legal rules, norms, and organizations together with characteristic patterns of
interrelation between it and other societal institutions.[122]

The primary concern of the sociology of law is
the analysis and understanding of the legal system
as such rather than the mere recognition of legal
aspects in selected areas of social life. Modern
sociology, in general, has neglected the study of
law even though several classical social theorists
gave legal phenomena an important place in their
analyses.[123]

There are several reasons why there is a gap
in efforts to develop a comprehensive and systematic knowledge of the legal institution. Sociology
avoided the law because of a failure to recognize
sufficiently its social nature (i.e., theorists
viewed the legal system as a set of rules which
falls into the normative realm and also has been
thought to consist of a static body of pronouncements). Secondly, sociologists have directed their
research to behavior, ecology, and social disor-
ganization rather than to the legal issues

surrounding crime, delinquency, and social problems. They also placed much greater emphasis on
informal than on formal mechanisms of social
control (i.e., law) wrongly concluding that formal
sanctions are without any force or consequence
whatever.[124]

There are certain central themes and issues
in the sociology of law according to Schur. These
are: (1) law and its social context, (2) unifor-
mities and diversity in legal systems, (3) the
two-edged nature of law, (4) relation between
procedure and substance, (5) substantive and formal
rationality, (6) limitations on science of law, and
(7) sociology and legal policy.[125]

Law (even if viewed primarily as a set of
rules) is always an outcome of social processes
according to Schur. Law is not totally a dependent variable shaped by the social context in
which it occurs and without any significant shaping
force of its own. Law consists of two aspects,
freedom-enhancing and freedom-reducing which are
constantly combining within particular legal systems since an increase in the rights of some will
always entail some restrictions on the rights of
others. The essence of legality to some resides in
a system of dispute-resolving institutions that
adhere to a specified "adjudicative" model.[126]

The formalistic-substantive dilemma (i.e.,
based on Weber's concept that Western legal systems
rely chiefly on formal rationality which could
conflict with the desirable aspects of substantive
rationality) is relevant to the attempt to develop
a legal system that provides both equality before
the law and justice to individual cases; to the
need for a law system to simultaneously maintain a
consistent and flexible system under continuous
social change; and to maintain the formal character of rulings while using scientific knowledge

as an aid to judicial determination.[127]

The primary goal of sociology of law is systematic knowledge of legal systems. It cannot indicate what the goals of the legal system shall be since it can never prove values. Sociology of law theorists have formulated or accepted a particular definition of law or of legal. Such efforts by both classical and contemporary theorists leave one with a confusing variety of alternative definitions. Schur thinks it would be a mistake to single out any one definition and label it "the definition", but he does state that law in American society consists of the rules established by legislatures, or courts, or backed up by sanctions imposed by courts.[128]

The need for formal mechanisms of social control as exemplified in legal institutions may be closely related to the nature and effectiveness of informal social controls (i.e., the sanctioning of norms through informal group processes). The differences in dominant forms of social control are the hallmark of the distinction between Gemeinschaft and Gesellschaft. Sometimes informal control replaces unworkable legal control.[129]

We know that mechanisms of social control are required in all societies. The problem is one of determining whether or when a particular type of control mechanism (i.e., legal) is necessary. Thus the problem is one of distinguishing law from other social norms. Despite the variety among legal definitions, a consensus has emerged to the effect that all societies have something we call law.[130]

Since the time when Malinowski confused custom and law, a number of theorists took pains to distinguish custom from law in terms of the source of sanctions and enforcement (i.e.,

individuals and groups in the case of custom and
the central authority of the society in the case
of law). Law as the central authority of the
society at large becomes in practice the administration of state power. Schur points out that
the definitions of law of Radcliffe-Brown, Hoebel,
and Weber all emphasize enforcement through
central authority while Selznick, Hart, and
Bohannon develop balanced concepts of law recognizing the element of centralized authority and
also stressing the special qualities of obligation intrinsic to legal phenomena (i.e., stressing
the concept of authority).[131]

The meaning of law can also be approached
from the standpoint of the basic functions served
by legal institutions. Schur lists the four
functions of law stated by Hoebel, and examines
the four problems that must be solved before a
legal system can provide the integrative function
proposed by Parsons.[132]

Ronald L. Akers

Akers in his article, "The Concept of Law"
reviews some of the major concepts of law found in
the literature. His purpose is to introduce some
of the classic and recent formulations of law as
a way of obtaining a perspective on important
issues in the concept of law. The purpose is not
to present a comprehensive review of the place
definitions and theories of law have occupied in
the history of sociology of law.[133]

Law is initially considered as social control
through legitimized coercion, and this is considered as the dominant concept. There is widespread
agreement that law is part of society's control
system, that the legal system is not coterminous
with the whole system of social control, that law

is just one type of social control, and that law
is a normative system (i.e., a system of rules
about the way people should behave and the atten-
dant sanctions). The dominant theme is that legal
norms are backed by some form of legitimized or
authoritative coercion or force.[134]

Law is secondly seen as a system of rules
made and enforced by the sovereign political
community. The form which this legitimized force
takes in definitions of law is that of the political community (i.e., sense of a governmental
unit exercising control over a territory and
recognizing no higher secular sovereignty). Such
conceptions can be traced to the Austinian
philosophy of positive law. Ross, Sumner, Pound,
Davis, Harvey, Chambliss, and Seidman hold this
view of law.[135]

Thirdly, law is seen as the assumed basis for
or predictions of authoritative decisions. The
emphasis in sociological jurisprudence is on the
law as it is actually carried out and enforced
rather than law as a series of rules contained in
statutes. Holmes and Cardozo's definitions of
law typify this approach. Anthropologists such as
Schapera and Pospisil also use authoritative decisions for the basis of law.[136]

Coercive definitions of law and the problem
of stateless societies and international relations
is the fourth category analyzed by Akers. Barkun
believes that primitive societies and the world
community represent cases of legal order without
sanctions. Primitive societies and the international community do not lack means of coercion,
rather they lack the ultimate monopolization of
authorized force by a political entity. Further
if the conceptual requirement be dropped that the
use of legitimized force in support of norms be
in the hands of a political state, then a

definition of law can be devised which includes
many stateless societies and the norms of international relationships. Such definitions have
been devised by Llewellyn, Hoebel, Weber, and
Gibbs.[137]

Noncoercive definitions view law as authoritative decision and procedure and constitute the
fifth category of legal definitions. Some writers
reject legitimized coercion (whether or not backed
by the political state) as a defining characteristic of law. Coercive definitions restrict law
to only that legitimized coercion which is applied
in a regular and systematic way. Noncoercive
definitions retain and elaborate on the criterion
of authorization and proper procedure. They tend
to stress the way in which rules are made and
applied rather than the content of the sanctions
enforcing conformity or settlement of disputes.
Such definitions have been devised by Kantorowicz,
Hart, Fuller, Selznick, Ehrlich, and Timasheff.
Akers also examines law in private groups and
associations as a part of noncoercion definitions.[138]

Akers states that all of the definitions of
law (five categories) agree that law is a form of
social control and consists of social norms. All
definitions agree that a system of norms enacted
and enforced by the coercive power of the modern
political state is law, and that law can be
distinguished in this way from other societal
normative systems. There is some disagreement
among definers about how law differs from other
parts of the social control system in stateless
societies and from other phenomena that are
similar to law in many respects (i.e., internal
order of private organizations). The dominant
theme in making this distinction is the use or
threat of coercion in a regularized way by
authorized persons, whether or not these are
agents of the political state.[139]

Those definitions that reject coercion as a
criterion of law place emphasis on authoritative
decisions that distinguish between primary and
secondary norms (i.e., those that directly relate
to personal conduct and those that specify how
authorized persons who react to primary norm
violations should behave).[140]

Coercive definitions include the requirement
that sanctions be applied for norm violation or to
enforce a dispute settlement in a systematic or
socially approved (i.e., normative) way by
socially approved agents. Coercive definitions
identify primary norms which qualify as law by
the requirement that their breach be met or
decisions about them be made in a way and by
persons who are authorized by secondary norms to
do so.[141]

Akers concludes that every conception of law
must recognize that both primary and secondary
norms are involved. In no concept has the defining characteristic of law been located in the
content of the primary norms of law as all refer
to the secondary norms or the agents and actions
governed by them. Lastly Akers defines law as
social control exercised by the political community and ultimately backed by coercive sanctions.[142]

Notes to Chapter I

1 Eugene Ehrlich, Fundamental Principles of
the Sociology of Law, Cambridge, Massachusetts:
Harvard University, Press, 1936, pgs. 473-479.

2 Ibid., 480-489.

3 Ibid., 493-489.

4 Ibid., 501-502.

5 Ibid., 504-505.

6 Eugene Ehrlich, The Sociology of Law,
Harvard Law Review, 36, no.2 (1922), pgs. 130-136.

7 Ibid., 137-140.

8 Ibid., 141-142, 144.

9 P.H. Partridge, Ehrlich's Sociology of
Law, In Studies In the Sociology of Law, Geoffrey
Sawer (ed.), Canberra: The Australian National
University, 1961, pgs. 1-2.

10 Ibid., 3-4.

11 Ibid., 5-6.

12 Ibid., 7-8.

13 Ibid., 9-10.

14 Ibid., 11-12.

15 Ibid., 13-14.

16 Ibid., 15-16.

17 Ibid., 17-18.

18 Ibid., 19-21.

19 Ibid., 22-26.

20 Max Weber, Law in Economy and Society,
edited with introduction by Max Rheinstein,
Cambridge, Mass: Harvard University Press, 1954,
pgs. xivii-li.

21 Ibid., liv-lix.

22 Ibid., lxii-lxvii.

23 Ibid., lxix-lxxi, 11-20.

24 Ibid., 41-45, 49-50, 56-59.

25 Julien Freund, The Sociology of Max Weber, New York: Random House, 1968, pgs. 245-249.

26 Ibid., 250-254.

27 Ibid., 255-260.

28 Ibid., 262-264.

29 Ibid., 265-266.

30 S.J. Stoljar, Weber's Sociology of Law, In Studies In the Sociology of Law, Geoffrey Sawer (ed.), Canberra: The Australian National University, 1961, pgs. 31-35.

31 Ibid., 36-40.

32 Ibid., 41-44.

33 Ibid., 45-48.

34 Ibid., 49-50.

35 Ibid., 51-52.

36 Karl Renner, The Institutions of Private Law, edited with introduction by O. Kahn-Freund, London: Routledge and Kegan Paul, 1949, pgs. 1-4.

37 Ibid., 5-9.

38 Ibid., 10-15.

39 Ibid., 16-20.

40 Ibid., 21-25.

41 Ibid., 26-30.

42 Ibid., 31-34.

43 Ibid., 35-38.

44 Ibid., 39-31.

45   Ibid., 42-43.

46   Geoffrey Sawer, Law As Socially Neutral: Karl Renner, In Studies In the Sociology of Law, Geoffrey Sawer (ed.), Canberra: The Australian National University, 1961, pgs. 137-140.

47   Ibid., 141-144.

48   Ibid., 145-151.

49   Ibid., 154-156.

50   Ibid., 157-160.

51   Huntington Cairns, Law and the Social Sciences, New York: Harcourt, Brace and Company, 1935, pgs. 125-128, 130-134.

52   Ibid., 136-142.

53   Ibid., 144-145.

54   Ibid., 157-161, 163-167.

55   Roscoe Pound, Sociology of Law, In Twentieth Century Sociology, Georges Gurvitch and Wilbert Moore (eds.), New York: The Philosophical Society, 1945, pgs. 297-314, 316-323.

56   Ibid., 325-332, 334-335.

57   Ibid., 337-340.

58   Nicholus S. Timasheff, An Introduction to the Sociology of Law, Cambridge, Massachusetts: Harvard University Press, 1939, pgs. 19-26.

59   Ibid., 27-35.

60   Ibid., 36-41.

61   Nicholas S. Timasheff, Growth and Scope of Sociology of Law, In Modern Sociological Theory in Continuity and Change, Howard Becker and Alvin Boskoff (eds.), New York: The Dryden Press, 1957, pgs. 424-426.

62   Ibid., 428-448.

54

63 Georges Gurvitch, Major Problems of the Sociology of Law, Journal of Social Philosophy, 6, no. 3 (1941), pgs. 198-200.

64 Ibid., 201-204.

65 Ibid., 205-208.

66 Ibid., 209-211.

67 Ibid., 212-213.

68 Ibid., 214-215.

69 William M. Evan, Introduction, Law and Sociology, New York: Free Press, 1962, pgs. 1-11.

70 F. James Davis, The Sociological Study of Law, In Society and the Law, F. James Davis et al., New York: Free Press, 1962, pgs. 3-16.

71 Ibid., 17-22.

72 Ibid., 23-28.

73 Ibid., 32-36.

74 F. James Davis, Law as a Type of Social Control, In Society and the Law, F. James Davis et al., New York: Free Press, 1962, pgs. 39-41.

75 Ibid., 42-44.

76 Ibid., 45-47.

77 Ibid., 48-50.

78 Ibid., 51-53.

79 Ibid., 54.

80 Ibid., 55.

81 Ibid., 56.

82 Ibid., 57.

83 Ibid., 58.

84 Ibid., 59-60.

85   Talcott Parsons, The Law and Social
Control, In Law and Society, William M. Evan
(ed.), New York: Free Press, 1962, pgs. 56-61.

86   Ibid., 62-66.

87   Ibid., 67-68.

88   Ibid., 69-70.

89   Ibid., 71-72.

90   Vilhelm Aubert, Researches In the Sociology of Law, The American Behavioral Scientist, 7
no. 4 (1963), pg. 16.

91   Ibid., 17.

92   Jerome Skolnick, The Sociology of Law in
America: Overview and Trends, Social Problems,
13, no. 1 (1965), pgs. 4-12.

93   Ibid., 13-25.

94   Ibid., 27-29.

95   Ibid., 30-32.

96   Ibid., 37-38.

97   Ibid., 39.

98   Geoffrey Sawer, Law In Society, London:
Oxford University Press, 1965, pgs. 7-9, 12-16.

99   Ibid., 23-26, 30-31.

100   Ibid., 46-47, 147-150.

101   Ibid., 165-166, 168-169.

102   Philip Selznick, The Sociology of Law,
In The Sociology of Law, Rita J. Simon (ed.),
Scranton, Pennsylvania: Chandler Publishing
Company, 1968, pgs. 190-194.

103   Ibid., 195-199.

104   Philip Selznick, The Sociology of Law, in
International Encyclopedia of the Social Sciences,
New York: Free Press, 1968, pg. 50.

105   Ibid., 51.

106   Ibid., 52.

107   Ibid., 53.

108   Ibid., 54.

109   Ibid., 55.

110   Ibid., 56.

111   Ibid., 57.

112   Ibid., 58.

113   Ibid., 58.

114   Paul Bohannon, Law and Legal Institutions, In International Encyclopedia of the Social Sciences, New York: Free Press, 1968, pg. 73.

115   Ibid., 73.

116   Ibid., 74.

117   Ibid., 74.

118   Ibid., 75.

119   Ibid., 75.

120   Ibid., 75.

121   Ibid., 77.

122   Edwin M. Schur, Law and Society: A Sociological View, New York: Random House, 1968, pgs. 4-6.

123   Ibid., 7-8.

124   Ibid., 10-11.

125   Ibid., 12-13.

126   Ibid., 14-15.

127   Ibid., 60-70.

128   Ibid., 71-73.

129   Ibid., 74-76.

130   Ibid., 77-78.

131   Ibid., 79-80.

132   Ibid., 81.

133   Ronald L. Akers, The Concept of Law, In
Law and Control in Society,   Ronald Akers and
Richard Hawkins (eds.), Englewood Cliffs, New
Jersey: Prentice-Hall, 1975, pgs. 5-6.

134   Ibid., 7.

135   Ibid., 8.

136   Ibid., 9.

137   Ibid., 10.

138   Ibid., 11.

139   Ibid., 12.

140   Ibid., 13.

141   Ibid., 14.

142   Ibid., 15.

Chapter II

Sociology of Criminal Law

Cesare Beccaria

Beccaria on the basis of his Essay On Crime
and Punishments is honored as one of the cofound-
ers of the sociology of criminal law along with
Bentham. He attacked the establishment (i.e.,
status quo) for its obsolete system of criminal
justice. The foundation of his theory of criminal
law is based on the social contract theory and
deals with the concept of legitimacy of law and the
right of punishment.[1] Beccaria enunciated the
principles that legislative law is above judge-
made law and that societal laws apply to everyone
on an equal basis.

According to Beccaria, judges should mediate
disputes as third parties but should have no right
to interpret criminal statutes. He feels that
clarity of the criminal law serves as a good crime
prevention technique while severe, cruel, and
inhuman punishment is a poor technique. Further
punishment should be used as both a crime control
and crime prevention technique since it has an
educative function. Punishment to be effective
must be prompt, and apply equally to all. In
addition penalties for law breaking must be long
term to be effective. Beccaria does not believe
in the death penalty as it does not serve as a
deterrent to crime.[2]

A crime classification scheme has been
devised by Beccaria which grouped crimes as those
against the state, against personal security of
property, and against disruption of public order.
Beccaria wants reform of criminal justice procedures. In particular he believes that one is

innocent until found guilty; evidence should be
made public; trials should be public; one should
be tried by his peers; and all offenders should be
treated as equal before the law.[3]

Jeremy Bentham

In his books, The Rationale of Punishment and
Theory of Legislation, Bentham develops an ethical
system of social control based on utilitarianism
(i.e., pleasure-pain principle). He specifies
several categories of social sanction such as
legal, political, moral, physical, and religious
in his concept of social control. A legal sanction is only effective if the majority of the
population adhere to it. Further only explicit
social controls can keep the average person from
becoming a criminal.[4]

The theory of crime control of Bentham states
the less certain the punishment the more severe it
must be if it is to have any deterrence potential,
and it is impossible to have equivalent punishment
for offenders because of variations in their back-
grounds. He adheres to a theory of crime causation that takes socialization into account. Thus
resocialization of potential offenders is the best
crime prevention technique. Also punishment is a
necessary evil since it aids in the resocialization process of offenders. Bentham advances the
hypothesis that the punishment should fit the
crime (i.e., the motivation of the criminal should
serve as a source for his type of punishment).
His theory of criminal behavior based on application of the pleasure-pain principle is logical in
theory but impractical to implement since it
assumes that all people rationally and consciously
contemplate their every action.[5]

Finally Bentham's sociology of law stresses
the need for reform of the criminal justice system, and like Beccaria he advocates that the law
function as a means to prevent crime. In particular Bentham stresses such reforms of the criminal
justice system as mitigation of severity of punishment, reformation of criminals, restructuring
of the jury system, abolition of debtor's prison,
abolition of certain statutes (i.e., those dealing
with usury and taxes), and reorganization of court
procedure.[6]

Gabriel Tarde

Tarde in his books, Penal Philosophy, Penal
and Social Studies, and Comparative Criminology
accepts a social-psychological theory of crime
causation. In particular he utilizes the concepts
of individual personality and social group relationships in formulating his crime causation
theory (i.e., the causal relationship between the
individual and the choices he makes in a given
environment).[7]

The influence of the social environment is
most significant in shaping criminal behavior as
crime results from this environment. Tarde
evolves his laws of imitation from studies of
criminal behavior, and thus saw the criminal as a
member of an occupational group or a profession.
His laws of imitation consist of the law of
fashion, of custom, and of substitution (i.e.,
insertion). Crime is explained simply by applying
the laws of imitation to it. Tarde analyzes the
crimes of vagrancy, drunkenness, and murder to
which he applies his theory of imitation.[8]

His theory of crime prevention concerns
itself with the theory of moral responsibility.
Tarde believes in the efficiency of punishment as

a crime prevention measure. Criminal responsibility rests on the social self and its relation
to both the cultural and subcultural contexts.[9]

Tarde attempts in an indirect manner to
classify crimes as rural and urban and thus deal
with crime from an environmental perspective
(i.e., his statement that city crimes are against
the person). His sociology of law deals with the
role of judges, use of expert witnesses to determine sanity of offenders, and reformation of
juries. Tarde's penology stresses early condi-
tional release for deserving inmates. He also
believes that punishment for a specific crime
should be the same for all offenders.[10]

Emile Durkheim

Durkheim, in his book <u>Division of Labor in
Society</u>, feels that crime is a necessary societal
component and its presence allows for the evolution of the criminal law. He maintains that the
kind and degree of punishment and the rationale
behind sanctions have varied according to societal
organizational structure (i.e., homogeneous undifferentiated and advanced differentiated urban
societal types).[11]

In the homogeneous undifferentiated type of
society, punishment is meant to protect and preserve social solidarity. Punishment is a mechanical reaction to preserve social solidarity, and
there is no concern with offender rehabilitation.
The wrongdoer is punished as an example to the
community that deviance will not be tolerated. In
the advanced and differentiated urban type of
society, punishment is focused upon the individual
and deals with restitution and reparations (i.e.,
harm done to the victim). Crimes are thought of
as acts which offend others and not the collective

conscience of the community. Punishment is eval-
uated in terms of what is good and proper for the
individual, and is therefore applied to the offender in order to reform him.[12]

Durkheim's concept of anomie is an attempt
to explain crime in the advanced and differentiated urban society. Heterogeneity and increased
division of labor weaken traditional societal
norms and the resultant social changes loosen
the social controls upon people allowing the
development of a cult of materialism and indivi-
dualism. This type of environment is condusive to
producing crime and antisocial behavior on a large
scale. Thus a society where social cohesion has
broken down and social isolation is great loses
its traditional social control mechanisms and
eventually suffers from a high rate of crime.[13]

Lunden and Gurvitch in separate essays concerning Durkheim's sociology of criminal law state
that Durkheim is concerned with the relation
between forms of sociality (i.e., solidarity) and
kinds of law found in societal types. Accordingly
penal law corresponds to what Durkheim calls
mechanical solidarity (i.e., Gemeinschaftlike
society) while family, contractual, commercial,
administrative, and constitutional law correspond
to organic solidarity (i.e., Gesellschaftlike
society). Law arising from mechanical solidarity
is accompanied by repressive sanctions while law
arising from organic solidarity is accompanied by
restitutive sanctions.[14]

Equality, liberty, and justice as legal
concepts evolved with the rise of organic solidarity according to Durkheim. The modern state is an
equalitarian association of collaboration that
favors contractual relations and affirms individual
law. Durkheim also concerns himself with the
relations between forms of sociality (i.e.,

solidarity) and kinds of law found in different
legal systems. Thus he has studied different
types of societies utilizing anthropological data
and has attempted to correlate the development of
a particular legal system with the development of
a particular societal type.[15]

Pedro Dorado Montero

Lopez-Rey in his article on Montero states
that the latter thinks the criminal law should
not be used to punish offenders but should offer
effective moral and social protection to them.
Thus Montero is positivistic in his orientation
to the criminal justice system and the criminal
law. He advocates social change in the administration of justice system for he feels there is
a basic struggle between society and the individual where the latter is at a distinct disadvan-
tage. A conflict oriented criminal justice system cannot correct the offender's criminal behavior, only punish him. Thus the judge who
represents society can only punish while the
offender has only himself and his standing in the
community as a defense. The criminal justice
system therefore should adopt the treatment (i.e.,
therapeutic) model and stress crime prevention
over crime control. The function of the court
should switch from punitive orientation to a
rehabilitative orientation. This switch would
allow utilization of specialists who could aid
the court decide on proper correctional procedures
and programs for offenders.[16]

Montero is firmly opposed to labelling individuals as criminals since this is damaging to the
rehabilitative process. He believes in the use of
the indeterminate sentence for offenders and flex-
ibility of treatment practices. Thus all correctional techniques including penal sanctions

should be utilized in the attempt to rehabilitate all offenders according to Montero. Such concepts as amnesty, pardon, etc. should be abolished and in their place should be substituted treatment centers in order to insure that each offender will be properly and completely rehabilitated.[17]

C. Ray Jeffery

Jeffery in his essay, "Criminal Justice and Social Change" states there is a basic dilemma between the Classical (i.e., legal reform) school and the Positive school (i.e., scientific criminal study) branches of criminology as the former school defines crimes in legal terms and examines it as a legal entity while the latter school (which dominates American theory) rejects the legal definition of crime and examines it as a psychological entity. The classical school defines crime within the strict limits of criminal law while the Positive school attacks the legal definition of crime and replaces it with sociological definitions of law.[18]

The rejection of the legal definition of crime has left sociologists with no agreement as to what is crime. Thus some sociologists believe that crime should be defined as antisocial behavior while a minority still adhere to a legal definition which has been resurrected by those theorists concerned with the sociology of criminal law. Most criminologists according to Jeffery are not interested in the sociology of criminal law since they are crime control oriented (i.e., have a reform orientation) and as positivists are concerned with the scientific solution of social problems (ala Comte), not truly understanding social events (ala Weber).[19]

The Positive school seeks an explanation of crime in the criminal, not in the criminal law. Thus most criminologists seek a universal category of behavior that can be explained in terms of a theory of behavior and not in terms of legal definitions of crime. These theorists have developed an incomplete theory of criminal behavior which is not really a crime theory according to Jeffery. The Positive school is concerned with the doctrine of determinism, and the assumption is made that the criminal law holds the individual responsible for his conduct. Thus the Positive school stresses the importance of the criminal over the crime and consequently evaluates behavior solely as psychological while omitting completely the sociological determinants of behavior.[20]

Law is a measure of social rather than individual responsibility and assumes that individuals are responsible for their actions. Further the law evaluates behavior and establishes norms of conduct. The criminal is one who has been judged by the group to have violated the code of conduct and deserves to be punished. The Positive school in its psychiatric orientation is potentially in conflict with the criminal law since the psychiatrist is not interested in the meaning of crime and punishment, only in the criminal. Thus mental illness is not defined as a violation of codes of conduct.[21]

The Classical school punishes the man for the crime (i.e., a definite penalty for each crime) while the Positive school states that the punishment must fit the criminal (i.e., stresses individualized treatment and protection of society against the criminal). Positivists have ignored the criminal law and have abandoned the traditional legal safeguards (i.e., law protects society against the individual and simultaneously

the individual against arbitrary actions of the
state). The entry of positivism into criminal
law theory has created an untenable position
wherein the legal rights of juvenile, alcoholic,
drug addict, and the mentally ill are ignored in
the name of treatment according to Jeffery.
Positivists view punishment in the context of its
meaning to the offender rather than its meaning
to society (i.e., use of indeterminate sentence,
parole, probation, suspended sentence, and good
time laws).[22]

Positivistic criminology rejects the legal
concept of crime and accepts the concept of
individualized justice; rejects the concept of
punishment and accepts the concept of treatment;
and rejects the study of criminal law but accepts
the study of the individual offender. Thus the
Positive school studies the offender independent
of the criminal law and with little concern for
the legal process by which crimes are created.
Positivists would like to ignore the deterrent
aspect of the criminal law in favor of the rehabilitative aspect. Jeffery is an advocate of the
Classical school and rejects the prevalent argu-
ment that criminology should be independent of the
criminal law as the latter must be a major part of
criminology to his way of thinking.[23]

In his essay, "The Historical Development of
Criminology" Jeffery writes about the evolution of
criminal law in society. Starting with anthropological data, Jeffery states that early anthropologists found it difficult to differentiate
between law and custom in traditional societies.
All law was either custom or no law existed in
primitive society. These classical theorists
believed that all primitive law was private law;
that the kinship group enforced sanctions against
the offender in the form of a blood feud; and
only later was the feud replaced by payment of

compensation. Only when traditional society
evolved to the state of urban-industrialism did
private law change to public law. Jeffery
utilizes Maine's classic, <u>Ancient Law</u>, to deal
with legal evolution in ancient societies.

Through the English historical example,
Jeffery traces the development of the public law
(i.e., familial law to state law or kinship system
based law to feudal law). First evolved the
appeal which was settled by trial by battle. This
type of legal self-help was followed by the indict-
ment that was resolved either by trial by ordeal
or by jury. During the Middle Ages as the commercial revolution progressed, the law of wrongs
developed into the law of crimes and the law of
torts. The criminal law in particular developed
during this period as a means of meeting the
problems created by the commercial-urban revolution (i.e., creation of laws of vagrancy, poverty,
and theft).[25]

Criminal procedures slowly changed from
arbitrary judge-made decisions to strict legal
definitions of crimes as put forth in statutes
passed by parliament. The accusatorial (i.e.,
Anglo-American) and inquisitorial (i.e., Roman)
criminal procedure systems evolved, the former
system being a private matter while the latter is
the concern of the state. Further the accusatorial systems demands procedural safeguards for
the offender while the inquisitorial system
denies basic civil rights to the defendant.[26]

According to Jeffery, two basic theories of
justice evolved in the last three centuries.
These are the retributive theory whose purpose is
to punish, not deter or rehabilitate; and the just
punishment or deterrence theory whose purpose is
to deter future criminal misconduct. The Positive
school substitutes scientific categories of

behavior for legal categories, substitutes
treatment for punishment, and accepts punishment
as retributive.[27]

The Positive school defines crime as unde-
sirable antisocial behavior (i.e., accepts deviance as criminal rather than law breaking as
criminal). The Positivists confuse crime and
criminal behavior since they reject the legal
definition of crime. Recent developments in
Positivistic criminology have been the social
welfare influence upon criminals and juvenile
court practices and procedures and the psychiatric
impact on the criminal law. The social welfare
influence upon both criminal law and juvenile
court procedures has resulted in denial of basic
constitutional rights of the offender. Jeffery
criticizes the psychiatric approach as providing
no evidence that mental disease causes criminal
behavior. Freudian theory (i.e., behavior
determined by inner forces of psychic phenomena)
is the one considered by the legal profession
and the courts despite the fact that the Classical school argues that behavior is determined
by its consequences (i.e., utilizing reinforce-
ment theory) according to Jeffery.[28]

Gilbert Geis

Geis in his articles, "Sociology, Criminology, and Criminal Law" argues that sociological
theory has contributed very little to criminologists' understanding of law while very little
criminological theory has contributed to sociologists' thinking about legal control or criminal
behavior systems. Thus one finds that criminal
law and criminology are peripheral to the main
current of legal and sociological theory respec-
tively in general, and sociology of law has had

little influence on both criminology and sociology
in particular.[29]

Criminology by long association with sociology is more concerned with the causes of behavior than with its consequences. Rather than
emphasizing criminal law, criminology emphasizes
the deviant behavior and social problems
approaches. Thus criminology has paid too much
attention to crime definitions which are not
based on a legal foundation since sociological
theorists have not been interested in the criminal
law which they neither created nor control.[30]

Hills

Law is not defined by Hills who accepts the
conclusions of interest-group theorists that
criminal laws change as the interest-power
structure of society changes. Thus criminal law
definitions change and are adapted to the changes
of the societal social order.[31]

Hills states there are two competing major
theoretical perspectives to the sociology of
criminal law: the value-consensus and interest-
group theories. The value-consensus position
states that criminal laws reflect those societal
values which transcend the immediate, narrow
interests of various individuals and groups, ex-
pressing the social consciousness of the whole
society. The legal process thus regulates, har-
monizes, and reconciles all conflicting claims to
enhance the welfare of the social order.[32]

The interest-group position states that
criminal laws will change with modification in the
interest-power structure of society. As societal
social conditions change, the criminal law will
adapt to these changes in the distribution of

power of various interest groups. Interest-group
theorists emphasize the ability of particular
groups to shape the societal legal system to serve
their needs and safeguard their interests.[33]

Sociology of criminal law to Hills is an
analysis of conflicting moral codes and interests
caused by an absence of societal consensus which
is kept alive by strong and powerful interest
groups which influence legislation and its application on a society-wide basis.[34]

Turk

Turk in his book Criminality and the Legal
Order accepts the conflict perspective on the law
as the most relevant for sociology of criminal law.
He perceives legality as an attribute of whatever
words or deeds are defined as legal by those able
to use to their advantage the machinery for making
and enforcing rules. Political power then determines legality.[35] Law is directly related to
social conflict in society according to Turk. A
law is a set of words about behavior, either describing what people actually do or specifying
what they ought to do.[36] Legality depends upon
the ability of some social groupings jointly to
seize upon the mechanisms for creating, maintaining, changing, and destroying laws. For those
powerful enough to have some impact on the legal
process, law will be viewed as compromise. For
those who have no power in the struggle to control
legal mechanisms, law will assume the form of
edicts.[37]

The focus in sociology of criminal law should
be upon patterns of conflict (i.e., overt and
covert). This focus is between different kinds of
social groups who manifest different value-atti-
tude systems. Society is composed of authorities

(i.e., those holding dominant, decision-making positions) and subjects (i.e., those holding subordinate positions). Legal norms vary in regard to the proportion of a population affected according to Turk. Thus subjects can be distinguished from authorities by their inability to influence the processes of norm creation or enforcement.[38]

There is an attempt by Turk to construct a theory about authority-subject conflict over legal norms and about the conditions under which subjects are likely to be criminalized in the course of conflict. He states that the study of criminality is the analysis of relations between the statuses and roles of legal authorities (i.e., creators, interpretors, and enforcers of right-wrong standards in society) and those of subjects (i.e., acceptors or resistors but not makers of such standards).[39]

The legality of norms according to Turk depends upon how they are defined by authorities. A norm is a law if the authorities say that it is (i.e., they are prepared to use force to make people comply). The ultimate legal norm is the rule that the final decision of the authorities is binding. If the expectations of the authorities regarding their legal treatment of subjects is unclear, there is room for normative conflict to arise.[40]

In an authority relationship the control ordering of the parties should be clear as both authorities and subjects should continue to perform their roles in a way that the relationship does not become either too coercive or too consensual. Obvious and repeated failure by the authorities to sanction violators of any legal norms constitutes inadequate role performance and contributes to weakening the authority structure over time.[41] The increasing estrangement of

authorities and subjects can be reversed only if
the authorities exercise restraint in dealing with
the norm-violators. The law is an instrument of
order no matter how receptive the authorities are
to making legal changes. Should the authorities
fail to achieve conditioning of norm violators,
there will be an eventual dissolution of the
social order, a period of explicit power struggles,
and establishment of a new social structure in
which new groupings have emerged and take their
places in the new power struggle.[42]

Chambliss

Law is defined by Chambliss and Seidman as
not merely a body of rules but as a dynamic process involving every aspect of state action, for
this action involves either creation of a norm,
adjudication about its content, adjudication that
has been violated, or a sanctioning process. This
set of processes comprises the law.[43]

In his writings, Chambliss refers to the
consensus model or theoretical approach to law and
society as the value-expression hypothesis and to
the conflict model as the interest-group hypothesis.[44] In 1971, he renamed the two models of law
and society value-consensus and value-antagonism.[45]
In 1973 Chambliss refers to the models as positivist (i.e., functionalist) and conflict.[46] In
1975 he has updated his 1969 theoretical viewpoint
and reutilizes the terms consensus and conflict
models in reference to the legal system of society.[47] Here Chambliss refers specifically to both
structural-functional and conflict perspectives.[48]

Sociology of criminal law is presently
dipolar in theoretical orientation according to
Chambliss. The functionalist view states that
acts are defined as criminal because they offend

the moral beliefs of society. Those who violate
the criminal law are punished according to prevailing mores of society. Individuals are labeled
criminal because their behavior exceeds tolerance
limits set by the community. The lower classes
are more likely to be arrested because they commit
more crimes. Criminal law becomes more restitutive
rather than repressive (i.e., penal) as society
becomes gesellschaft. The conflict view states
that acts are defined as criminal because it is to
the interest of the ruling class. Ruling class
members are able to violate the laws while members
of the subject classes will be punished. Individuals are labeled criminal because it is in the
interest of the ruling class regardless of community tolerance. The lower classes are labeled
criminal more often because the bourgeoisie's
control of the state protects them from stigma-
tization. As capitalist society becomes more
gesellschaft and the gap between the bourgeoisie
and proletariat widens, penal law will expand in
an effort to coerce the proletariat into sub-
mission.[49]

With respect to the sociology of criminal law,
the consensus and conflict models of society
present quite different fundamental assumptions
according to Chambliss. The consensus model
emphasizes the shared interests of everyone in
society and the consensus over fundamental values
which this shared interest creates. The conflict
model emphasizes the role of conflicts between
social classes and interest groups as the moving
force behind the creation and implementation of
criminal laws.[50]

Chambliss lists the theories derived from the
consensus perspective. There are theories that
see the law as a reflection of "perceived social
needs" which reasonable men agree must be met if
society is to continue; theories that see the

criminal law as an expression of what is in the
"public interest"; theories that perceive the law
as a reflection of the "moral indignation" of a
particularly influential segment of society; and
theories that see the law as an expression of the
most fundamental values that are inherent in
society.[51] Chambliss also lists the theories
derived from the conflict perspective. There are
theories that emphasize the role of "moral entre-
preneurs" (i.e., groups that organize to achieve
legal changes which they think are essential for
societal well-being); theories that emphasize the
importance of bureaucratic interests in the
rationalization of problems that are inherent in
society; theories that emphasize the conflicts
that inhere between interest groups competing for
the favors of state power; and theories that
emphasize the inherent conflicts between those who
rule and those who are ruled and who perceive the
criminal law as incorporating rules for enforcing
the interests and ideologies of the ruling
classes.[52]

The structural-functional perspective has
dominated sociology of criminal law for many years
according to Chambliss. The basic assumption of
this perspective is that the criminal law is a set
of rules stipulated by legislatures and courts
which reflect societal beliefs. This perspective
also sees the criminal law as fulfilling certain
basic societal needs. The problem with this
perspective is its failure to specify whose interests, views, and needs are being satisfied by the
societal legal system. The emergent perspective
in sociology of criminal law is the one emphasizing social conflict as the moving force behind
the criminal law in action. The social relations
which are part of the class, labor, and productive
systems of capitalist societies are viewed as more
important in determining the content and functioning of the criminal law process than are societal
values, norms, and beliefs.[53]

Richard Quinney

In his book, <u>Crime and Justice in Society</u>
Quinney feels that the most significant developments in modern criminology have been the awareness
of the criminal law and inquiries into its foundation, enforcement, and administration. This
statement is based on the knowledge that criminal
law only rarely studied by criminologists despite
the fact that Classical school theorists defined
crime strictly in legal terms. This was due to the
influence of the Positive school theorists who
adopted a nonlegal conceptualization of crime.
Only a small group of criminologists since the
1930's (i.e., Michael, Adler, Tappan, Vold, Jeffery,
and Turk) have called for a sociological analysis
of the criminal law. These theorists feel that
crime should be studied within the framework of
the criminal law.[54]

Quinney reviews the evolution of the criminal
law in English society. The concept of criminal
law emerged only when the custom of private vengeance was replaced by the principle of harm to the
whole community when any member was injured.
Criminal law developed only after the achievement
of political unity which allowed the establishment
of a centralized government that could administer
the law universally. In turn the common law
evolved as the king's power grew and criminal
statutes evolved (i.e., laws of theft and vagrancy) in response to societal needs created by
socio-economic changes in society. American law
developed from the common law traditions of England
although tinged by a puritanical morality (i.e.,
Prohibition, sexual psychopath laws, and drug
laws).[55]

Behind all law formulation are special
interest groups who stand to benefit. Criminal

laws are formulated to promote the interest of
certain societal groups. Administration of the
criminal law is political and extra-legal considerations are commonplace. Thus the criminal
justice process is discretionary, caters to special interests, and is influenced by socio-economic considerations.[56]

Criminal law theory has not been developed
despite considerable research on the topic over
the years. Legal theory and sociological theory
are as far apart today concerning the sociology of
criminal law as they were in 1912. Quinney turns
to Pound's theory of interests as a possible
point of convergence for the legal theorists and
sociological theorists to rally around. Despite
Pound's theorizing, research on the role of interests in formulating and administering the law has
been nonexistent. Quinney feels that Pound's
theory of interests is based on a consensus model
of law that operates in a pluralistic society, and
accordingly law adjusts and reconciles conflicting
interests.[57]

A sociological theory of interests is presented by Quinney to provide a theoretical perspective for presenting and interpreting research
in the sociology of criminal law. His theory
postulates that law is created by interests,
assumes a conflict-power model of society, and
proposes a conceptual scheme for analyzing the
relationship between law and interests. A number
of propositions are put forth by Quinney in support
of his interests theory. First, law consists of
specialized rules that are created and interpreted
in politically organized society. Second, this
type of society is based on an interest structure.
Third, this interest structure is characterized by
unequal distribution of power and by conflict.

Last, the law is formulated and administered
within the interest structure of politically organized society.[58]

Quinney in his book, Crime and Justice in
America takes up where he left off in his analysis of criminal law from previously published
material. He states that since 1970, a body of
empirical research has been developed on the
sociology of criminal law but most of it has been
positivistic and directed toward explaining how
laws are formulated, enforced, and administered
rather than devoted to questions about why law
exists, whether law is necessary, or what constitutes a just and equitable legal system. Even
Neo-classical (i.e., social constructionist)
theorists avoid a critical analysis of the contemporary legal system, fail to analyze the legal
order from a non status quo perspective, and
conform to the existing social order conception
of the legal institution. Thus contemporary
sociology of criminal law accepts and supports
the existing legal order. It also analyzes the
legal system in terms of the existing social order.
Therefore there has been no critique of the legal
order of advanced capitalist society in the
sociology of criminal law.[59]

A critical theory of criminal law that is
based on a Marxist perspective and understanding
of the legal order is advocated by Quinney.
According to his critical theory, law in capitalist society gives political recognition to
powerful social and economic interests. The legal
system provides the mechanism for the forceful
and violent control of the majority in society.
The state and its accompanying legal system
reflect and serve the needs of the ruling class.
Awareness that the legal system does not serve
society as a whole is Quinney's starting point

for what he calls a critical understanding of law
in capitalist society.[60]

The goal of a critical theory of criminal law
is to demystify crime and justice in society.
Quinney states his critical theory in a syllo-
gistic fashion. His theory starts with the statement that the American state is based on an advanced capitalist economy organized to serve ruling
class interests. Criminal law is an instrument of
both the state and the ruling class who use it to
maintain and perpetuate the existing social and
economic order. The contradictions of advanced
capitalism require that the subordinate classes
remain oppressed, especially through the coercion
and violence supplied by the legal system. Criminal law will be increasingly used in an attempt
to maintain domestic order as capitalist society is
increasingly threatened by oppressed people who
are abused by the elitist oriented criminal law.[61]

Charles E. Reasons

In his book, The Criminologist: Crime and the
Criminal Reasons states that the study of crime has
been mostly of criminals, not the criminal law. He
feels there is a need for studies dealing with the
emergence of criminal laws within a socio-his-
torical context. Further criminologists have not
been concerned with the sociological study of law
but with crime control.[62]

The various schools of jurisprudence in
general and the sociological jurisprudence of
Pound in particular are discussed by Reasons. He
deals with Quinney's social reality of crime
theory of interests, and Quinney's critical theory
of criminal law. Reasons criticizes Quinney's
theories stating that all states whether capitalist

or socialist have legal systems that serve some
interests more than others. He faults Quinney
further since the latter does not demonstrate that
socialist society has a legal system that is
equalitarian. Reasons does feel that Quinney
demyths the American legal system on this particular issue.[63]

Finally Reasons examines the concepts of
victimless crimes and of overcriminalization. He
feels it is important to analyze the law and its
agents as independent variable in the creation and
maintenance of criminal behavior. Crime may be
viewed as phenomena created by special interests
who with their definition of rightness to triumph
and become the laws of society.[64]

Edwin M. Schur

Schur in his book, Our Criminal Society feels
that criminal sanctions are not necessarily appropriate to every effort at social control. Attempts
to employ criminal law to regulate morality ultimately face difficulties in society. Legal and
sociological theorists have stated that criminal
laws that do not have the support of the dominant
societal social norms are limited in their effectiveness.[65]

American criminologists have focused on
individual causation and have not concerned themselves with what the criminal law should be. This
is in contrast to the findings of the British
Governmental Committee on Homosexual Offenses and
Prostitution which broke ground with its conception
of the role that criminal law should play in
society. The Committee places the burden of jus-
tifying applications of the law on those who seek
to impose such control over the behavior of individuals.[66]

Sociologists are now beginning to look more directly at the socio-legal problems of societal reactions to deviance according to Schur. There is a growing recognition that the criminal law is the inappropriate means to deal with deviance. These crimes without victims are unenforceable laws that attempt to legally proscribe the willing exchange of socially disapproved but demanded goods or services (i.e., homosexuality, drug addiction, prostitution, gambling, etc.). These types of crimes involve a consensual transaction or exchange and no direct and clear harm is inflicted by one person against another so no complaint is lodged. Some criminal laws that deal with victimless crimes produce more social harm than good, cause a great deal of immorality, throw the legal system into disrepute, and allow organized crime to grow and prosper.[67]

According to Schur, we rely upon a criminal solution to all social problems and thus criminalize situations that do not concern the criminal justice system. There has been overlegislation in the area of deviance (i.e., sexual behavior, vice, and political white collar crimes). Political behavior should be designated a crime only if it constitutes a distinct threat to social order (i.e., Nixon era abuses). Schur also feels that many juvenile statutes and court procedures represent an overextension of the crime-defining process since they deal with behaviors which are non-criminal (i.e., ungovernability, waywardness, and incorrigibility) and violate due process of law guarantees of the Constitution.[68]

Jack P. Gibbs

Gibbs in an essay, "Crime and the Sociology of Law" criticizes criminologists who tend to employ a statutory criterion of criminality (i.e.,

who accept the idea that crime is an act so designated by a statute). As inadequate the statutory conception of crime is, alternative definitions of crime are not easily formulated largely
because many of the attributes commonly ascribed
to crimes are dubious. Gibbs examines some alternative solutions to statutory designations of
crime such as violations of conduct norms, social
evaluation of crime, and the analytical approach
to crime.[69]

The proposal by Sellin that criminology
abandon the concept of criminal law and study
conduct norms is inadequate for the sociology of
criminal law. The evaluation of acts which are
distinguished by the character of public reaction
to them as crime is difficult to deal with since
crime definitions are neither right nor wrong.
The analytic approach utilizes Sutherland's
differentiae of crime which seeks a generic
definition of crime from the common features of
acts statutorily designated as crime. Sutherland
defines crime as any conduct which is contrary to
criminal law. Criminal law is defined from its
essential characteristics - politicality, penal
sanction, specificity, and uniformity. Gibbs
finds fault with this definition when applied to
other than American culture.[70]

Any definition should recognize that crimes
are acts contrary to criminal law and not laws in
general. Further Gibbs states that before one can
formulate a definition of criminal law, one must
define law in its generic sense. He selects
Weber's definition of law. Law to Gibbs is an
evaluation of conduct held by at least one person
in a social unit; that these members of the social
unit on their own initiative or at other's request,
will use their special status to attempt by
coercive or noncoercive means to revenge, rectify,
or prevent behavior that is contrary to the

evaluation with a low probability of retaliation
by persons other than the individual(s) at whom
the reaction is directed.[71]

Gibbs applies his legal definition to
several traditional societies and concludes that
his definition applies universally. He applies
his definition to the criminal law where it is
found not to provide a solution to the crime
definition problem unless one distinguishes
criminal law from tort and contract law.[72]

Akers

Akers in his book Law and Control in Society
states that the central theoretical issue in the
study of law and society is the nature of interrelationships between law and other institutions
and normative systems in society.[73] In examining
law in the political state, Akers reviews what
he calls the two major models or theoretical
approaches to understanding modern politically
organized society (i.e., consensus or conflict).
The first of these theories states that the law
evolves from normative consensus in society and
serves the broad interests and functions of
society as a whole. The second theory views law
as formed out of the conflict of values and actions
of various groups in society and reflects the
narrow interests of societal groups which wield
economic, social, and political power.[74]

After a review of the literature that
includes the writings of several theorists, Akers
states that most evidence is in support of the
conflict model. He notes that the law supports
the norms of groups who have been politically
successful in society. It is accepted as fact
that the law is most often the outcome of group
conflict. More important to Akers is whether

the nature of group conflict can best be described
as due to either the power elite or pluralistic
concepts.[75]

Akers states that neither the pluralistic nor
power elite concepts deny the importance of power,
domination, and conflict in society. He also feels
that either model (i.e., pluralistic or power elite)
more closely fits reality than a consensus model.
But admitting the primary importance of power and
conflict should not deny a place for the consensus
model of law in society. Akers states there can be
little doubt that the core of the criminal law is
designed to protect the life and property of everyone although differentially enforced against the
less powerful in society. He concludes that
powerful groups in society make the law reflect
their interests to a great extent but the law also
reflects the views of all of society at any given
time.[76]

Sociology of criminal law to Akers is an
analysis of the consensus and conflict approaches
to society. In particular he deals with the
conflict model where he reviews both pluralistic
and power elite concepts. He concludes that the
societal legal system reflects both special
interests as well as areas of concern to everyone
(i.e., victimless crimes, public interest laws,
and regulatory statutes). Akers feels that law is
both shaped by and has an independent impact on
society; grows out of, is influential upon, and is
consistent with conspicuous normative structures.[77]

Notes to Chapter II

1 Elio Monachesi, Cesare Beccaria, In
Pioneers in Criminology, Hermann Mannheim (ed.),
Montclair, New Jersey: Patterson Smith, 1972,
pgs. 38-41.

2 Ibid., 42-43.

3 Ibid., 44-47.

4 Gilbert Geis, Jeremy Bentham, In Pioneers
In Criminology, Hermann Mannheim (ed.), Montclair,
New Jersey: Patterson Smith, 1972, pgs. 53-56.

5 Ibid., 57-61.

6 Ibid., 62-66.

7 Margaret Wilson Vine, Gabriel Tarde, In
Pioneers In Criminology, Hermann Mannheim (ed.),
Montclair, New Jersey: Patterson Smith, 1972,
pgs. 292-294.

8 Ibid., 295-297.

9 Ibid., 298-300.

10 Ibid., 301-302.

11 Emile Durkheim, Division of Labor in
Society, New York: Free Press, 1964, pgs. 68-80.

12 Ibid., 81-110.

13 Ibid., 111-132.

14 Walter Lunden, Emile Durkheim, In Pioneers
in Criminology, Hermann (ed.), Montclair, New
Jersey: Patterson Smith, 1972, pgs. 390-393;
Georges Gurvitch, Sociology of Law, London:
Routledge & Kegan Paul, 1947, pgs. 83-89.

15 Walter Lunden, Emile Durkheim, In Pioneers
in Criminology, Hermann Mannheim (ed.), Montclair
New Jersey: Patterson Smith, 1972, pgs. 394-397;
Georges Gurvitch, Sociology of Law, London:
Routledge & Kegan Paul, 1947, pgs. 90-96.

16   Manuel Lopez-Rey, Pedro Dorado Montero,
In Pioneers in Criminology, Hermann Mannheim (ed.),
Montclair, New Jersey: Patterson Smith, 1972,
pgs. 401-404.

17   Ibid., 405-408.

18   C. Ray Jeffery, Criminal Justice and
Social Change, In Society and the Law, F. James
Davis et al., New York: Free Press, 1962, pgs.
264-270.

19   Ibid., 271-276.

20   Ibid., 277-281.

21   Ibid., 282-287.

22   Ibid., 282-287.

23   Ibid., 296-304.

24   C. Ray Jeffery, The Historical Development
of Criminology, In Pioneers in Criminology,
Hermann Mannheim (ed.), Montclair, New Jersey:
Patterson Smith, 1972, pgs. 459-464.

25   Ibid., 465-471.

26   Ibid., 472-480.

27   Ibid., 481-489.

28   Ibid., 490-498.

29   Gilbert Geis, Sociology, Criminology, and
Criminal Law, Social Problems, 7 (1959), pgs.
40-43.

30   Ibid., 44-46.

31   Stuart Hills, Crime Power, and Morality:
The Criminal-Law Process in the United States,
Scranton, Pennsylvania: Chandler Publishing
Company, 1971, pg. 5.

32   Ibid., 3-4.

33   Ibid., 4-5.

34 Ibid., 6.

35 Austin Turk, Criminality and Legal Order, Rand McNally, Chicago, 1969, pgs. 30-32.

36 Ibid., 36.

37 Ibid., 32.

38 Ibid., 33.

39 Ibid., 35.

40 Ibid., 37-38.

41 Ibid., 43 & 45.

42 Ibid., 46-48.

43 William Chambliss & Robert Seidman, Law, Order, and Power, Reading, Massachusetts: Addison-Wesley Publishing Company, 1971, pg. 9.

44 William Chambliss (ed.), Crime and the Legal Process, New York: McGraw-Hill Company, 1969, pgs. 8 & 10.

45 William Chambliss & Robert Seidman, Law, Order, and Power, Reading, Massachusetts: Addison-Wesley Publishing Company, 1971, pgs. 17, 40, 45-46, 53-54.

46 William Chambliss, Functional and Conflict Theories of Crime, New York: MSS Modular Publications, Module 17, 1973, pgs. 1-23.

47 William Chambliss (ed.), Criminal Law In Action, Santa Barbara, California: Hamilton Publishing Company, 1975, pgs. 5-6.

48 Ibid., 476-477.

49 William Chambliss, Functional and Conflict Theories of Crime, New York: MSS Modular Publications, 1973, Module 17, pgs. 1-23.

50 William Chambliss (ed.), Criminal Law In Action, Santa Barbara, California: Hamilton Publishing Company, 1975, pg. 5.

51 Ibid., 6.

52 Ibid., 6.

53 Ibid-, 476-477.

54 Richard Quinney, Crime and Justice in Society, Boston: Little, Brown and Company, 1969, pgs. 1-9.

55 Ibid., 10-16.

56 Ibid., 17-21.

57 Ibid., 22-26.

58 Ibid., 27-30.

59 Richard Quinney, Criminal Justice In America, Boston: Little Brown and Company, 1974, pgs. 8-16.

60 Ibid., 17-21.

61 Ibid., 22-25.

62 Charles E. Reasons, The Criminologist: Crime and the Criminal, Pacific Palisades, California: Goodyear Publishing Co., 1974, pgs. 99-100.

63 Ibid., 101-102.

64 Ibid., 103-104.

65 Edwin M. Schur, Our Criminal Society, Englewood Cliffs, New Jersey: Prentice-Hall, 1969, pgs. 191-194.

66 Ibid., 195-201.

67 Ibid., 219-223.

68 Ibid., 224-227.

69 Jack P. Gibbs, Crime and the Sociology of Law, In Crime, Criminology, and Contemporary Society, Richard D. Knudten (ed.), Homewood, Illinois: The Dorsey Press, 1970, pgs. 397-398.

70 Ibid., 399-400.

71   Ibid., 401-402.

72   Ibid., 403-404.

73   Ronald Akers & Richard Hawkins (eds.), Law and Control in Society, Englewood Cliffs, New Jersey: Prentice-Hall, 1975, pg. 41.

74   Ibid., 43-44.

75   Ibid., 47.

76   Ibid., 48-49.

77   Ibid., 41.

Chapter III

Sociological Jurisprudence

Roscoe Pound

Pound in his multi-part article, "The Scope and Purpose of Sociological Jurisprudence" surveys the various schools of jurists and methods of jurisprudence in a very definitive manner. He defines and characterizes the analytical, historical, and philosophical schools of jurisprudence. The analytical school is comparative and deals with the study of the purpose, methods, and ideas common to developed systems of law. The historical school is also comparative and deals with the origin and development of law and legal systems. The philosophical school deals with both philosophical and ethical bases of law and legal systems.[1]

The social philosophical school starts the evolutionary process culminating with the sociological school. This school emphasizes political, economic, and general social science methodology and compares rules of one legal system with rules of another legal system using anthropological data to broaden its philosophical base. The next school to emerge is the social utilitarian school of Jhering who holds a social theory of law. Punishment to Jhering should be adjusted to the nature of the criminal. The neo-Kantian school is a return to the philosophical method. Stammler the spokesman for this school promotes a social justice philosophy, formulates a legal theory of social justice, and a theory of just decision of causes. The Neo-Hegelians under Kohler seek a proper place for law study and its relation to philosophy of law, economics, and anthropology.

89

The school has produced a theory of law as a product of culture and a theory of sociological interpretation and application of law. The Marxian
interpretation of law is utilized by Brooks Adams
who regards law as a manifestation of the will of
the dominant social class whose motivation is
economic.[2]

Sociological jurisprudence like sociology had
its origin in the positivist philosophy of Comte
and evolved through mechanical, biological, and
psychological stages to its present status according to Pound. The positivists typify the mechanical stage of sociological jurisprudence as they
analyze the legal system as it evolved and show
interest with the effects of social change on
societal legal structures. The biological stage
sees the end of law as giving free play in an
orderly and regulated manner to the elimination of
unfit cultures based on race (i.e., Spencerian
theories of legal evolution for various societies).
The psychological stage is based on analysis of the
social group and social psychological theories of
sanction and their effect on legal philosophy
(i.e., based partially on writings of Ward, Tarde,
and Gierke).[3]

Pound concludes by stating that sociological
jurisprudence is based on a comparative study of
legal systems, legal doctrines, and legal institutions. It deals with analysis of the social facts
upon which the law must proceed and to which it is
applied.[4]

Braybrooke in his analysis of Pound's sociological jurisprudence mentions the latter's definition of law as a highly specialized form of
social control carried on in accordance with a
body of authoritative precepts applied in a judicial and administrative process. The purpose of
law is social engineering according to Pound.[5]

A thesis of the five stages of legal development is proposed by Pound. The stages consist of the primitive (i.e., law as an instrument for peace keeping); strict (i.e., law as the prevailing agency to regulate society); equity (i.e., ethical solution to legal controversies); maturity (i.e., equality and security in property and contract rights); and socialization (i.e., maintenance or furtherance of society).[6]

The jural postulates of Pound are based on Kohler's writings and reflect justice and right which civilization presupposes. Of the seven jural postulates, the first five have been derived as generalizations from the course of legal development, while the remaining postulates reflect an attempt to detect what the community expects from civilization.[7]

The theory of interests of Pound examines the multiplicity of human claims or demands which exist in society. These individual claims, wants, or demands to have something or to do something (coercively or voluntarily) are called interests. Interests are classified as individual, social, and public. Individual interests are those involved immediately in ones life and are asserted in title of that life; social interests are those involved in social life in society and asserted in title of that life; and public interests are those involved in life in a politically organized society and asserted in title of that organization. The task of law is recognizing and securing certain of these interests within defined boundaries imposed by the effectiveness of legal action and the precepts, processes, and techniques of the law. The end of the law is to satisfy the maximum number of human claims, wants, and desires with the minimum of friction and waste. In order to achieve these claims, wants, and interests - they must be categorized as individual or social

and then competing interests weighed so that justice will be served.[8]

A program of sociological jurisprudence is
outlined by Pound which consists of several points
to enable jurists to take more cognizance of the
social facts upon which law must proceed and to
which it is to be applied in actual situations.[9]

Benjamin Cardozo

Aronson and Gurvitch in their articles on
Cardozo's sociological jurisprudence state that
the latter recognizes that law is a social phenomena intimately related to all other aspects of
human life. Cardozo wants to preserve the stability of the law by organizing the considerable
conflicting decisions brought about in the pursuit
of stare decisis. The law follows a definite body
of general rules which can not be altered by judge
or legislative body according to Cardozo. Further
the law is a body of relatively stable rules and
standards having prior existence to the decisions
of any court. Thus law is relative since courts
constantly proclaim that previous law is not true
law on the basis of appealing to the body of
doctrine and traditions of the Anglo-American common law. Cardozo does not feel that law can be
reduced to socially sanctioned custom and attempts
to remain out of the Malinowski/Radcliffe-Brown
dispute as to the nature of law.[10]

The courts are the product of the state and
its power according to Cardozo. But the state in
promulgating laws cannot overlook the habits and
customs of the community. He feels that judges
should have a more active role in the legal institution and become law makers in addition to law
interpreters. Four mutually related and supple-
mentary principles guide the judge in his efforts

to develop the law. These principles are the
philosophical, evolutionary, traditional, and
sociological.[11]

The first three principles serve as guides to
the judge to enable him to make the law conform to
cultural norms. The law should be constant and
stable but not to the point where it becomes dysfunctional (i.e., laws that serve their purpose
should be retained, those that do not should be
modified or rescinded). Utilitarian principles
should apply to all legal rules.[12]

The sociological principle is the most important one for jurisprudence as it serves as the
means whereby the juristic system is restrained
from lagging too far behind the social needs and
ideals of the contemporary social order. The
purpose of sociological jurisprudence is to correct
the lag between law and culture. Within the limits
of jurisprudence and taking into consideration
societal mores, law changes to conform to changes
in the societal social system. Conflicting values
from differing subcultures within society have to
be sorted utilizing the mores as the source and
criterion of legal hypotheses. Law like other
values is a cultural phenomenon which has to be
interpreted by judges who should be social philosophers according to Cardozo. But the quality of
judge-made laws is affected by the regulation of
the court as an organ of the state (i.e., Warren
Court versus Berger "Nixon" Court).[13]

Karl N. Llewellyn

In his book entitled, _Jurisprudence_ Llewellyn
deals with the lack of cooperation between lawyers
and sociologists. The former deal with rules of
law and legal doctrines which are outside the
sociological realm. Sociology thus has not

accomplished much in the law field since Weber
according to Llewellyn. Law analyzed from the
institutional perspective can be understood by
both legal and sociological theorists. One must
analyze the legal institution by examining its
conduct, interaction, norms, standards, and rules.
By analysis of these concepts, one can see that
the legal institution is characterized by vari-
ability and impermanence (i.e., a human institution, not one of rules alone).[14]

The legal institution according to Llewellyn
deals with law and order as well as law and government. Thus there is a basic interaction of men
acting under and within rules, and under and within
a tradition of goodwill and expertise. Llewellyn
describes the functions of the legal institution
in terms of what he calls "law-jobs". There are
four law-jobs: (1) cleaning up of trouble-cases;
(2) channeling of conduct, habit, and expectation
in such fashion as to prevent or reduce the
emergence of such trouble-cases; (3) re-channeling
conduct, creating new habits and expectations
appropriate to changing conditions of personnel or
group life without creating new trouble-cases; and
(4) allocating the authoritative say and regulating
the manner of its saying, in case of emergency, of
doubt, or of innovation.[15]

There are also two sub-jobs within the legal
institution according to Llewellyn. First there
is organizing and directing the law team through
effective leadership and administration. Second
there is the development, maintenance, and im-
provement of craft know how among the specialists
engaged on other law-jobs. There are in addition
lesser legal-governmental institutions (i.e.,
regulative law) and buttressing institutions
which are only partly legal-governmental. Last
there are buttressing not-primarily-legal machin-
eries such as the family and the economy.[16]

All members of the legal institution (i.e., judge, counsellor, advocate, legislator, policy-shaping administrator, and administrative assistant) perceive and use the official rule-stuff differently. Thus there should be a mutual understanding of different roles and role-relationships within the institution to make it function better according to Llewellyn.[17]

Following Weber's analysis of the concept of bureaucracy, Llewellyn feels that the concept of craft-and-craftsmen should be used as a working tool in the law-and-government bureaucracy. A law-craft is a recognizable line of work practiced by recognizable craftsmen. Law-work is not a single craft since a particular lawyer may practice more than one law-craft (i.e., advocate, counsellor, and legislator). Llewellyn analyzes the various craft-jobs in the law-and-government institution. The appellate judge applies "ought-rules" to reviewing trial court decisions and thus must sustain, reverse, or solve law problems and create new law interpretations. The trial judge uses the imperative aspect of the official law. The advocate utilizes the law as a tool of persuasion within the limits of the law. The last craft-job is the legislator who uses the law for shaping the conduct of the people in society.[18]

Gurvitch in his analysis of Llewellyn's sociological jurisprudence states that the latter believes that the sociology of law serves as the only basis of jurisprudence. Law is defined as that which the officials do about disputes. Sociology of law must take the different societal institutional subcultures into account as well as the role of particular groups in the life of the law. Thus sociology of law must study the legal aspect of every social institution, not just the court and the state.[19]

Such key concepts as law-ways, law-stuff, the
legal, and law-jobs are examined by Llewellyn.
Law-ways are any behavior or practice distinctly
legal in character, flavor, or effect. Law-stuff
is any phenomena in the culture which relate discernably to the legal. This includes rules of law,
legal institutions of any kind, lawyers, law-
libraries, courts, habits of obedience, a federal
system, and anything else in the culture whose
reference is discernably legal. The legal is the
patterned normative regularity in the law-ways and
the law-stuff (i.e., consisting of a projection
and idealization of right patterns of different
degrees in precision and generality from any
group). The law-jobs (i.e., a juridical technique)
consists of the disposition of trouble cases; in
the preventive channeling, in the allocation of
authority, and the arrangement of procedures; and
in the net organization of the group or society as
a whole so as to provide direction and incentive
to the group or society.[20]

Julius Stone

Stone in his book, Law and the Social Sciences
defines sociological jurisprudence as the study of
the relationship of the legal order with the wider
social order. The interrelations involved include
the influences of extralegal elements of the social
order on the formation, operation, change, and
disposition of the legal order, as well as the
influence of the legal order on these extralegal
elements. Stone maintains that sociological
jurisprudence cannot evolve into sociology of law.
His reasons for this are that sociologists are
likely to encounter formidable obstacles in handling legal materials; that law by its nature cuts
across almost all the social sciences; and legal
education so far has seen no pressing need to

analyze the legal institution in relation to other
societal institutions.[21]

Sociological jurisprudence applies equally to
analysis of past as well as contemporary legal
systems; deals with the law and social change;
addresses itself to the influences of social, economic, and psychological factors on the law process
and law institution; seeks to bring social science
knowledge to help solve legal problems; and is
concerned with the effect of theories of justice
on the legal order.[22]

The rise of the school of sociological jurisprudence is traced by Stone from its origins in
both historical jurisprudence and sociology/
anthropology. He traces the origins of the field
to Savigny, Maine, and Montesquieu; followed by
the influence of Comte and Spencer's social
Darwinian ideas; the psychological influences of
Gierke, Ward, and Tarde culminates in the influence of Durkheim. Marx, Weber, Renner, and
Ross also have been influencial on the 20th
century theorists. Pound's American sociological
jurisprudence builds upon all who preceded him
and rivals the work of such European theorists as
Ehrlich, Duguit, and Hauriou.[23]

Parson's book, The Social System is used as
an analytical tool for examining the legal institution by Stone. Some of Parson's ideas are useful
for jurisprudence despite the involuted and eso-
teric language used according to Stone. Further
neither Parsons nor those discussing his writing
have made any significant contributions from the
juristic perspective as the Social System omits
the legal aspect from discussion. Stone substitutes the words, "legal order" for Parson's
"social system to create a framework that theorists of sociological jurisprudence can understand
(i.e., it is the structure of the relations

between the actors as involved in the interactive process which is essentially the structure of the legal order).[24]

A fault of Parson's theory of society is that it depends on the central notion of equilibrium (i.e., a stable dynamic society that does not suffer any traumatic change or breakdown). Another fault of the theory is that the equilibrium notion downgrades the actualities of conflict and coercion by using such consensus terms as "adaptation" and "integration".[25]

Hans Zeisel

Zeisel in his essay, "Sociology of Law, 1945-55" really outlines the growth of interest in both sociological jurisprudence and sociology of law in the United States. He characterizes the major American contribution to sociological jurisprudence as inquiries into the actual workings of the legal system and into the effects of legal rules upon those institutions immediately involved as well as eventually upon society in general (i.e., Supreme Court decision of 1954 concerning school desegregation). Further governmental and semi-public administrative agencies, legislative investigative committees, and grass roots organizations have all been instrumental in furthering the evolution of sociological jurisprudence in America.[26]

All this interest in sociological jurisprudence began with the theoretical writings of Pound, followed by those of Cardozo and especially Llewellyn. The features of the American legal system aided turning theory into research and finally into practice as shown by the studies conducted over the years in judicial reasoning and decision-making (i.e., at the appellate level) and the use of experiment in socio-legal inquiries (i.e., Chicago Law School projects of the 1950's).[27]

Hall

Hall in his book Theft, Law, and Society has attempted to determine the relationship between legal changes and value changes in society through an analysis of the law of theft. He expresses four theories concerning sociology of criminal law; (1) the functioning of courts is related to accompanying cultural needs. This applies to both procedural and substantive law. (2) Legal change follows a definite order. First a lag occurs between the substantive law and the social needs of society followed by an attempt by judges, officials, and the laymen to make adaptations (i.e., use of legal fictions). The last step in legal change is the enactment of new legislation to eliminate the lag. (3) Technicality and legal fiction function both to link the old law to the new and as to solutions of societal legal problems between social orders. (4) Sociology of criminal law is represented by the "law process" of the norm-oriented and directed conduct of large sectors of a societal population.[28]

Sociology of criminal law to Hall is an analysis of social structures, processes, and institutions of society. Criminal law represents a sustained effort to preserve important social values from serious harm and do so not arbitrarily but in accordance with rational methods directed toward the discovery of just ends.[29] Hall has analyzed the effects of legal and socio-economic change upon society and has demonstrated how changes in society are possible without rapid alterations of the law.

Gilbert Geis

In his article, "Sociology and Sociological Jurisprudence: Admixture of Law and Lore" Geis states that Pound's theory of sociological jurisprudence has seen little change over the decades although sociological theory has evolved significantly since the time of Small and Ross. Law and sociology in the early 20th century together created sociological jurisprudence since both fields shared an interest and an understanding of the classical continental writers and their theories. Unfortunately law is well established but sociology in trying to gain an identity in the United States broke with European theorists with the notable exception of Durkheim and Weber. Thus American sociological theorists downgraded involvement with legal theorists and lost touch with the legal institution leaving only a few European legal scholars to pursue an interest in sociological principles. No one paid much attention to Pound and his call for renewed ties between the two fields so sociological jurisprudence became of little interest except to a handful of sociologically oriented American jurisprudents.[30]

Geis reviews the relationship between jurisprudence and sociology starting with Pound and his relationship with Ross, Ward, and Small. Holmes was not impressed with these sociological theorists as Pound and was reluctant to accept any sociological theory as worthwhile and meaningful. Pound tried to tie the development of sociological jurisprudence to the growth of sociological theory but failed for the most part. The former field stayed speculative while the latter became more analytical and descriptive, stressing a small groups approach to an institutional approach.[31]

From the 1920's until after World War II only two works appeared in the field of sociology of law, Timasheff's book and that of Gurvitch, both European trained and oriented. Neither American philosophers of law nor sociological theorists accepted these works so sociological jurisprudence and sociology of law continued separate theoretical paths until the 1950's when sociologists of law began again to study the legal institution along narrowly defined lines of interest.[32]

Allen

Allen in <u>The Borderland of Criminal Justice</u> feels that the concentration of interest on the nature and needs of the criminal law has resulted in an absence of concern about the nature of crime. The behavioral scientist has all but forgotten how to deal with the types of behavior that should be declared criminal.[33] Allen states there has been a systematic lack of attention to the substantive criminal law which is due to the Positivist bias against authoritative rules in any form and even challenges the reality of such rules. Instead of considering the law as a set of rules or authoritative norms, Positivists have considered the law as a process according to Allen.[34] Interest has shifted from dealing with substantive law problems and definition of crime to dealing with procedural law and enforcement problems. Thus the systematic disconcern in the law of crimes has not stopped the enthusiastic enactment of penal laws which has created the problem of over-criminalization in our society. Allen refers to both offenses that affect or are believed to affect the security of the state as well as those crimes created by legislatures in large numbers to effect certain objectives of economic regulation or public welfare (i.e., regulatory offenses).[35]

Hart

Law is conceived by Hart in his book The
Concept of Law as having a certain quality not because it fits some abstract standard relating to
the values which it expresses but because of its
formal utterance by a body of certain sort (i.e.,
an organ of the state).[36] Hart states law consists
of particular kinds of rules. The essence of a
legal system lies in the union of primary and
secondary rules. Primary rules are informal rules
of obligation through which the basic conditions
of social existence are satisfied while secondary
rules are formal and clarify, authorize, and
empower.[37]

Secondary rules consist of rules of recognition which clarify what the authoritative primary
rules are and order them in a hierarchy of importance. They are also considered as rules of
change which authorize the introduction of new
primary rules. Last, secondary rules are adjudi-
cators which empower individuals to make authoritative determinations whether a primary rule has
been broken on a particular occasion.[38]

Sociological jurisprudence to Hart is an
analysis of primary and secondary norms. This
distinction is central to his concept of law
according to Akers.[39] Hart has developed a balanced concept of law that takes cognizance of the
concept of centralized authority and also stresses
the special qualities of obligation intrinsic to
legal phenomena.[40] Finally Hart assumes the
existence of specialized social institutions which
can be perceived as legal.[41]

Fuller

In The Morality of Law Fuller views law as
the purposive enterprise of subjecting human conduct to the governance of rules.[42] He insists
that the internal morality of law is neutral
toward its substantive aims although denying that
it is possible to conceive a system of law at
once faithful to the imperatives of legality and
indifferent to justice and human welfare.[43]

Fuller's eight criteria of legality presupposes that the central concern of the law ought
to be its predictability. To assume that the
primary value to be realized by law is predictability of the action of state organs is to assume a
common set of values for all.[44] He points out the
ways in which it is possible to fail in the
creation and maintenance of law. A system that
does not fail in meeting these criteria is considered law.[45] The criteria are (1) having no
rules at all so that only ad hoc decisions reign;
(2) making rules unknown or unavailable to those
who are expected to obey them; (3) creating retro-
active rules; (4) failing to have rules which can
be understood; (5) having contradictory rules;
(6) having rules which the affected individuals
are incapable of following; (7) making such fre-
quent changes in the rules that the persons subject
to them cannot properly orient their conduct with
regard to them; and (8) lacking congruence between
the rules as announced and the same rules as they
are administered or enforced.[46]

Sociological jurisprudence to Fuller is an
analysis of the internal principles of a rule system which can be considered the basic requirements
for law.[47] Fuller infers that the law is a neutral,
value-free framework within which conflict can be
adjudicated. The authoritative standards of the
legal system all conflicts to be resolved without
the need to make value-choices and thus no need
to choose between conflicting rules.[48]

Notes to Chapter III

1 Roscoe Pound, The Scope and Purpose of
Sociological Jurisprudence, Harvard Law Review,
14, no. 8, 15, no.1, and 15, no. 6 (1911-1912),
page. 489-500.

2 Ibid., 501-516.

3 Ibid., 140-168.

4 Ibid., 591-619.

5 E.K. Braybrooke, The Sociological
Jurisprudence of Roscoe Pound, In Studies in the
Sociology of Law, Geoffrey Sawer (ed.), The
Australian National University, Canberra, 1961,
pgs. 57-61.

6 Ibid., 62-67.

7 Ibid., 68-74.

8 Ibid., 75-83.

9 Ibid., 84-95.

10 Moses J. Aronson, Cardozo's Doctrine of
Sociological Jurisprudence, Journal of Social
Philosophy, 4, no. 1 (1938), pgs. 5-17; Georges
Gurvitch, Sociology of Law, Routledge & Kegan
Paul, London, 1947, pg. 132.

11 Moses J. Aronson, Cardozo's Doctrine of
Sociological Jurisprudence, Journal of Social
Philosophy, 4, no. 1 (1938), pgs. 18-26; Georges
Gurvitch, Sociology of Law, Routledge & Kegan
Paul, London, 1947, pg. 132.

12 Moses J. Aronson, Cardozo's Doctrine of
Sociological Jurisprudence, Journal of Social
Philosophy, 4, no. 1 (1938), pgs. 27-35; Georges
Gurvitch, Sociology of Law, Routledge & Kegan
Paul, London, 1947, pg. 133.

13 Moses J. Aronson, Cardozo's Doctrine of Sociological Jurisprudence, Journal of Social Philosophy, 4, no. 1 (1938), pgs. 36-44; Georges Gurvitch, Sociology of Law, Routledge & Kegan Paul, London, 1947, pg. 134.

14 Karl N. Llewellyn, Jurisprudence, University of Chicago Press, Chicago, 1962, pgs. 352-357.

15 Ibid., 358-360.

16 Ibid., 361-362.

17 Ibid., 363-366.

18 Ibid., 367-371.

19 Georges Gurvitch, Sociology of Law, Routledge & Kegan Paul, London, 1947, pgs. 135-139.

20 Ibid., 140-144.

21 Julius Stone, Law and the Social Sciences, University of Minnesota Press, St. Paul, 1966, pgs. 3-17.

22 Ibid., 18-26,

23 Ibid., 27-31.

24 Ibid., 32-39.

25 Ibid., 40-48.

26 Hans Zeisel, Sociology of Law, 1945-55, In Sociology In the United States of America, Hanz Zetterberg (ed.), UNESCO, New York, 1956, pgs. 56-57.

27 Ibid., 58-59.

28 Jerome Ha-1, Theft, Law and Society, The Bobbs-Merrill Company Inc., Indianapolis, 1952, pgs. xii-xiii.

106

29   Jerome Hall, General Principles of Criminal Law, The Bobbs-Merrill Company, Inc., Indianapolis, 1947, pg. 1.

30   Gilbert Geis, Sociology and Sociological Jurisprudence: Admixture of Law and Lore, Kentucky Law Journal, 52 (1964), pgs. 267-277.

31   Ibid., 279-282.

32   Ibid., 284-293.

33   Francis Allen, The Borderland of Criminal Justice: Essays in Law and Criminology, University of Chicago Press, Chicago, 1964, pgs. 29 & 31.

34   Ibid., 125.

35   Ibid., 126-130.

36   William Chambliss & Robert Seidman, Law, Order, and Power, Addison-Wesley Publishing Company, Reading, Massachusetts, 1971, pg. 48.

37   H.L.A. Hart, The Concept of Law, Oxford University Press, London, 1961, pgs. 78-79.

38   Ibid., 77-96.

39   Ronald Akers, The Concept of Law, In Law and Control in Society, Ronald Akers and Richard Hawkins (eds.), Prentice-Hall, Englewood Cliffs, New Jersey, 1975, pgs. 13-14.

40   Edwin Schur, Law and Society: A Sociological View, Random House, New York, 1968, pgs. 70-73.

41   Ibid., 75.

42   Lon Fuller, The Morality of Law, Yale University Press, New Haven, Connecticut, 1964, pg. 106.

43   William Chambliss & Robert Seidman, Law, Order, and Power, Addison-Wesley Publishing Company, Reading, Massachusetts, 1971, pg. 43.

44 <u>Ibid.</u>, 44.

45 Ronald Akers, The Concept of Law, In <u>Law and Control In Society</u>, Ronald Akers and Richard Hawkins (eds.), Prentice-Hall, Englewood Cliffs, New Jersey, 1975, pg. 13.

46 Lon Fuller, <u>The Morality of Law</u>, Yale University Press, New Haven, Connecticut, 1964, pg. 39.

47 Ronald Akers, The Concept of Law, In <u>Law and Control In Society</u>, Ronald Akers and Richard Hawkins (eds.), Prentice-Hall, Englewood Cliffs, New Jersey, 1975, pgs. 12-13.

48 William Chambliss and Robert Seidman, <u>Law, Order, and Power</u>, Addison-Wesley Publishing Company, Reading, Massachusetts, 1971, pg. 45.

Chapter IV

Anthropology of Law

<u>Henry Sumner Maine</u>

Maine in his book, <u>Ancient Law</u> traces the
evolution of theories of jurisprudence from the
Glossators who founded modern jurisprudence in
Italy in the 11th and 12th centuries to Blackstone
in England. His main theme is that all writings
from the aforementioned period are based on the
Roman conception of the law of nature. Maine
analyzes the theories of jurisprudence of
Montesquieu and Bentham as typical Age of Reason
analyses. He feels that theories of jurisprudence
take no account of the evolution of the law in any
given society over time. Knowledge concerning
ancient legal institutions can be gained from an
examination of ancient law and traditional societies.[1]

A comparison of contemporary legal systems
with ancient legal systems is made by Maine using
comparative anthropological data. The application
of comparative jurisprudence to primitive society
leads to the formulation of the patriarchal theory
of law. Maine states that the family was the basic
unit of ancient society while the individual is the
basic unit of modern society. Further the evolution of the basic unit from family to individual
can be found in an analysis of ancient law.[2]

An ascending series of groups out of which
the state appears (i.e., from family to house/gens
to tribe to commonwealth/state) is traced by Maine.
He states that the family is the key to the com-
prehension of primitive jurisprudence. The evolution of Roman law is selected for analysis by

Maine since it evolved slowly and clearly. He
undertakes a detailed analysis of the Patria
Potestas (i.e., paternal authority and power) in
order to understand legal evolution. Maine extensively describes Roman kinship terms in order to
demonstrate that the entire modern law of persons
originated in these terms. In an interesting case
study, he traces the status of females in Roman
society from an initial subordinate position to
their blood-relations to their modern Victorian
era position (i.e., subordination to the husband).[3]

Using the annals of Roman law, Maine demonstrates how the legal concept of family evolved.
He also shows using the Roman legal example that
a society in which all the relations of persons
are summed up in the relations of family evolves
toward a society in which all the relations arise
from the free agreement of individuals. Society
which has its origins in the family is based on
status and slowly evolves to a society which
emphasizes the individual and is based on contract.[4]

William Graham Sumner

Sumner in his book, Folkways states that
social control institutions (i.e., legal, police,
military) evolve from the mores of the ruling class
who possess the collective power within society.
Only competing elites contest those who control
power, never the masses. Sumner has selected an
elitist theory of power and rejects the Marxian
doctrine that the masses control power. He also
rejects the Marxian notion that the elite and their
legal structure have produced an evil society whose
institutions should be abolished.[5]

All institutions, laws, and actions of legislation are products of the mores but the nature of
the circumstances and from what mores can only be

determined by historical analysis according to
Sumner. He theorizes on the development of such
societal regulations such as customs and taboos.
First there is codification, then enactments, and
finally legislation. In the last stage, mores are
"put under" police regulation or finally put into
the criminal law. The taboos and customs evolve
into prohibitions and punishments that are planned
as deterrents rather than instruments of revenge.
Sumner states that the mores of different societies
or social orders are characterized by greater or
less readiness to use enactments for societal
purposes.[6]

When folkways become laws, they have changed
their character and are distinguished from mores.
Laws are rational, practical, mechanical, and
utilitarian whereas mores are unformulated and
undefined. Acts under the laws are conscious and
voluntary while acts under the folkways are uncon-
scious and involuntary. Laws supercede the mores
whereas mores come into operation when laws become
dysfunctional. Last, mores cover areas of culture
where no laws or police regulations exist although
new laws and regulations are created out of old
mores as society changes over time.[7]

Robert H. Lowie

Lowie in his book, Primitive Society generally
accepts and is concerned with the theories of Maine,
especially the latter's comparison of traditional
and modern jurisprudence. Lowie states there is a
predominance of criminal law in early societies.
Thus most disputes concern the individual victim
and his kin versus the offender with no state
intervention. Further the offense of one group
against another group is handled on a collective
basis (i.e., blood feud) while an offense of one

individual on another member of his own group is
handled within the collectivity.[8]

Criminal intent is not as important in primitive law as punishment of the social group for the
criminal act of one of its members. Payment is
made to the victim's group to avert feuds between
both groups. Criminal procedure is more concerned
with feud prevention than exact guilt determination. Magico-religious means in the form of oaths
and ordeals help determine the truth in criminal
or civil matters.[9]

Lowie offers examples of "juridical cultures"
from several societies. He examines the Australian
Aborigines, Ifugao (Philippines), Eskimo, Plains
Indians, Polynesians (Samoans), and Africans
(Togoland and Uganda). His analysis of these cultures shows that most primitive communities recognize not merely wrongs inflicted by individuals
against other individuals which ultimately involve
their respective kin groups (i.e., law of torts)
but also recognize offenses that are outrages
against the entire community or those who represent
the entire community (i.e., law of crimes).[10]

In an article entitled, "Anthropology and Law",
Lowie reviews the contributions of Maine, Morgan,
and Kohler to the anthropology of law field. Using
Maine and Morgan as a starting point, Lowie outlines
the evolution of the state within traditional society. He partially disagrees with Maine and Morgan
on their theories of kin group authority and states
that the rise of some type of sovereignty or community power structure leads to a supreme law and
eventual rise of the state. Kohler was instrumental in his emphasis on studying the legal institution within its cultural context. Lowie believes
that Maine and Kohler have made the most important
early contributions to anthropology of law.[11]

The family formation and family descent system theories of Malinowski and Vinogradoff are discussed by Lowie. He concludes that family law leads to a consideration of the property concept. Theories of universal and individual ownership of real and personal property among traditional, hunting, gathering, and simple agricultural societies are explained as are rules of inheritance. Lowie concludes that rules (i.e., laws) of inheritance among traditional cultures are diverse and connected with other societal institutions. For an example, he states that inheritance tends to conform to the rules of descent where there is a definite clan system.[12]

Arthur S. Diamond

Diamond in his book, _Primitive Law_ critiques Maine's classic _Ancient Law_. He feels that primitive law is law from its earliest beginnings until the rise of the historical state, and one must deal with primitive law where Maine left it. Diamond summarizes Maine's theory concerning ancient law from his three stages of growth concept (i.e., by legal fictions, by equity, and by legislation). Thus the purpose of Diamond's book is to trace the history of early law and to deal with Maine's theory of same in particular.[13]

Criminal law origins are fully dealt with by Diamond. He states that the growth of central executive authority in the community shaped the development of both the law of crimes and of civil injuries. Any attempt to accurately define the distinction between criminal and civil wrongs is fraught with difficulty. The distinction between the two terms according to Diamond is that the sanction is enforced at the discretion of the state in case of a crime while in the case of a civil wrong enforcement is at the discretion of the adult parties involved in the trouble-case.[14]

The origin of the crime-tort distinction is of
great interest to Diamond. A crime is not so much
an offense against a community but that which at
some part time was regarded as an offense against
it and resolved to punish that category of offender.
Partly from Maine has been drawn the widespread
misconception that in primitive law, there is no
separation between crimes and torts. This distinction is universal according to Diamond from the
time when civil and criminal law originated in
primitive society until modern society evolved.[15]

A classification scheme for the different
periods of primitive law has been devised by
Diamond. It consists of the first hunters, second
hunters, first agricultural grades, second agricultural grades, third agricultural grades, early
codes (2200 to 1500 BC), middle codes (375 BC to
725 AD), and late codes (500 to 1100 AD).[16]

Rudimentary forms of criminal law exists before the evolution of courts. By the period of the
second hunters, the main crimes of the primitive
criminal law include witchcraft, incest, bestiality,
and sacral offenses. Primitive law does not confuse the concepts of crime and tort. Courts and a
law of torts appear by the time of the first and
second agricultural grades, and until the late
Middle Codes there is no difficulty in distinguishing a crime from a tort since no wrongs are
simultaneously civil and criminal. There is very
little criminal law in the codes. The sanctions
of the civil law are mainly monetary until well
into the time of the Middle Codes. Even by the
time of the Late Codes, there is not a complete
fusion of the criminal and civil law. From the
period of the Late Codes, one can distinguish
crimes from torts but it is of more theoretical
than practical importance.[17]

The history of primitive criminal law is
traced by Diamond's examination of various offenses
as they evolved in society. These are witchcraft,
incest, sacral offenses, and offenses against the
welfare of the community. All three types of
offenses are crimes found universally in all the
periods of the primitive law classificatory scheme.
Another group of crimes of the primitive law consist of various offenses against the welfare of the
community, and later with the rise of the state,
offenses against the King. Before the rise of
courts, a communal nuisance and danger could be
punished by the community. In the age of the
Codes, the crown classified these offenses as
disobedience to and a challenge to the king's
order and authority. These crimes are all
breaches of the peace (i.e., ambush, burglary, har-
boring outlaws, neglect of military service, and
treason). Homicide and theft become capital offenses by the time of the Late Codes.[18]

Diamond states that the criminal law began
moving away from the civil law in the Early Code
stage, and by the Late Codes both civil and criminal law are separate but parallel in evolution.
In societies where courts have not evolved, the
earliest form of civil law is the practice to
avenge homicide (i.e., self redress being the only
recognized sanction exercised). The civil law of
wrongs (i.e., torts) evolved out of disputes
arising from personal injuries and theft. The
fixing of sanctions was by redress, agreement, and
judicial decision. Sanctions of fixed quantity
were applied for each common wrong. These sanctions were mostly pecuniary in nature until the
Middle Codes.

There was no conception of damages in primitive law. All civil wrongs or torts were compro-
mised by consent. Primitive civil sanctions were
often greater in amount than the actual monetary

loss suffered. Primitive civil law disregarded
the absence of intention more often than did the
primitive criminal law.[19]

As tort law developed, the family and its
head occupied an increasingly prominent place in
the civil law. By the stage of the Late Codes the
family head is an appropriate judge in all cases
of wrongs committed between family members or by
a member against him (i.e., institution of patria
potestas).[20]

Diamond deals with what he calls the evolution
of the four great civil wrongs of the primitive
law: homicide, wounding, wrongful sexual intercourse (i.e., rape and adultery), and theft. Before the evolution of courts, the sanctions for
homicide were left very much at large; there were
no recognized sanctions for wounds or wrongful
sexual intercourse; and there was no law of theft.
The civil sanction for all these wrongs was typi-
cally pecuniary although death could be prescribed
for homicide and corporal punishment for theft.[21]

The four stages of legal evolution of the
civil and criminal law are described in detail by
his book, The Evolution of Law and Order. These
stages are: (1) before courts or trials (typified
by the Second Agricultural Grade societies); (2)
Early Codes (exemplified by the Code of
Aethelberdt); (3) Central Codes (typified by a
division of jurisdiction into ecclesiastical and
secular courts); and (4) Late Codes (exemplified
by the rise of litigation).[22]

In first stage communities, which are small
and homogeneous, the existing standard of social
conscience maintains orderly communal activity
according to Diamond. Public opinion and the norm
of reciprocity are very important factors for
maintaining an orderly community. The problem of

the conception of law is examined in cultures not
possessing courts. Diamond does not define custom
and reciprocity as law although these are present
in primitive society. He concludes there is no law
in stage one communities although there are a few
rules which are precursors to law such as the rules
relating to marriage (i.e., controlling incest,
descent, and inheritance).[23]

The second stage of legal evolution is typified by the English Code of Aethelberdt. Law is
intentionally created and changed in this stage and
coincides with the use of writing in a given culture. The Early Codes instruct judges as to which
judgment should be given in a specified area; new
judgments are prescribed by legislation; they deal
mainly with rules relating to civil injuries,
sanctions are pecuniary although they are evolving
toward criminal sanctions; and compensation for
every kind of wrong varies according to the status
of the injured party. Criminal offenses are much
the same as before the Early Codes as punishment
is still death and/or confiscation of the offender's property.[24]

The third stage is characterized by the dom-
inance of the church in the legal sphere (i.e.,
recording, legal usages, advising the king on legal
matters, serving on secular courts, and trying certain criminal offenses). The church tried defen-
dants for offenses against God which included
witchcraft, incest, bestiality, and adultery. The
church also tried the religious offense of heresy,
the offense of perjury at this stage of legal evolution, and dealt with the questions of marriage
validity and inheritance disputes.[25]

The law at this stage no longer denotes a
mere collection of judgments, an occasional statute, or anything just and customary. It now em-
braces a system of rules and principles which make

up a distinct, independent, and self-sufficient
institution to which all members of society are
subject.[26]

Homicide is now a criminal offense as is
theft in some circumstances. In addition to the
death penalty for homicide, confiscation of property, mutilation, and forced labor are used as
punishment. The list of criminal offenses has
expanded with the growth of government. The pecuniary sanction now varies according to whether a
killing is intentional or not. Banishment and
outlawry are imposed as a sanction for certain
criminal offenses. The institution of the sanctuary has become important.[27]

The fourth stage of legal evolution is characterized by an interest in and love of litigation
and an acute sense of right and wrong. This is the
stage where detailed and technical rules of legal
procedure and law have evolved. Civil suit becomes
a matter for the king's court with the procedure
consisting of the oath, the use of a surety to pay
the judgment fee, and the fine if found guilty.
The jury (i.e., neighbors) takes the place of trial
before chief and communal elders. The sanction for
intentional homicide is death as it is now a religious as well as a secular offense. The death
sentence replaces compensation to kin in lieu of a
life taken. Homicide is either a criminal or civil
offense depending on its type (i.e., intentional,
unintentional, or self-defense). The concept of
sanctuary no longer applies although there is in
use the pardon of the king and benefit of clergy.
These now apply to certain types of homicide and
felonies which are punishable by death and confiscation of property.[28]

Bronislaw Malinowski

In, Crime and Custom In Savage Society,
Malinowski traces the rise of primitive law as a
field of study through an examination of the
German school and the writings of Maine and Morgan.
These theorists assumed that the individual in
primitive society was completely dominated by the
social group and blindly adhered to the traditions,
public opinion, and commands of the community.
According to Malinowski, the early school of
anthropological jurisprudence used insufficient
and baseless assumptions to reach its sterile conclusions.[29]

Primitive law is the study of the various
forces which make for order, uniformity, and
cohesion in traditional society. Civil law is
defined as the positive law governing all the
phases of tribal life. The civil law consists of
a body of binding obligations kept in force by a
specific mechanism of reciprocity and publicity
inherent in societal structure. Law and legal
phenomena do not represent a societal institution
but rather an aspect of the culture. Law is the
result of the configuration of societal obligations.
Thus the rules of law are felt and regarded as the
obligations of one person and the rightful claims
of another. This is Malinowski's (reciprocity)
definition of primitive law. Further he states
that many social scientists (i.e., Maine, Durkheim,
and Lowie) assume that primitive law is all criminal law. Thus anthropological theorists need not
worry about analyzing any primitive civil jurisprudence according to Malinowski.[30]

Anthropologists of law assume that all custom
is law to the savage, and that he obeys custom
automatically and rigidly. These same theorists
state there is no civil law in primitive society.
There are crimes but no mechanisms of enforcement.

Religious sanctions, supernatural penalties, group
responsibility and solidarity, and taboo and magic
are deemed the main elements of primitive jurisprudence. Malinowski feels that these contentions
held by some theorists are either mistaken, partly
true, or place the reality of the matter in a
false perspective.[31]

In an introduction to the book, Law and Order
In Polynesia, Malinowski attempts to clarify
statements made in his own book on primitive law.
He states that early anthropological theorists
could not perceive the variety of legal arrange-
ments found in traditional societies. Law to them
was concerned with interests of the sovereign or
of the elite. This idea of law could only be
associated with developed institutions, codified
rules, and regulated court proceedings backed by
force. Thus the classic theory of primitive law
states that no law exists, only obedience to rules,
customs, or conventions. The closest thing to law
in traditional society according to the classical
theorists is punishment by the community of overt
breach of conduct (i.e., criminal law).[32]

This assumption of collective or automatic law
enforcement is maintained by Durkheim and followed
by Radcliffe-Brown. Malinowski cites Pound's
definition of law, and states that Radcliffe-Brown
following this definition concludes that traditional societies have no law although all have
custom supported by sanctions.[33]

Malinowski carefully picks apart the classic
theory of primitive law. He suggests that the
important things for anthropologists of law to
study is whether a rule is actually obeyed or not,
under what conditions it is valid, and what social
mechanisms cause its enforcement. Malinowski finds
difficulty in applying Pound's political influence
oriented definition of law to traditional societies

since custom dominates and is outside the pale of political influence.[34]

Admittedly some societies have no law but possess a combination of sanctioned and neutral customs according to Malinowski. He states that the binding force of law is derived from the structure of societal institutions which operate on the basis of the norm of reciprocity (i.e., duties and privileges of one group of persons toward another group. Reciprocity is one of the key elements in the dynamic mechanism of enforcement of laws in society. Another element of legal enforcement is what Malinowski calls the systematic incidence of legal obligations. Thus the mutual support of kinsmen and clansmen (including the law of vendetta and rules concerning cooperative duties of joint property) are based on friendship, ambitions, and pride in one's lineage. He analyzes the reciprocal duties of rank and power by examining the duties, obligations, and privileges of tribal chiefs.[35]

In general people keep to what custom/law bids them to do because they know that some day the same custom/law will entitle them to demand a counter-service. These mechanisms of legal validity are found applying to economic and familial activities within kinship groups or the community according to Malinowski.[36]

Title to real property is analyzed, and Malinowski concludes that there is a correlation between the mythical and legal ideas on the one hand and the economic activities on the other hand which form the substance of communal land tenure. The study of kinship with emphasis on the family helps one comprehend the principle of reciprocity and of the systematization of claims and obligations. Malinowski feels that the legal study of marriage has been distorted in two ways. First the institution has been examined only in a sexist

manner, and second the act of marriage has not been
regarded as a legal transaction (i.e., legal part-
nership).[37]

Finding a solution to the primitive law problem is of crucial concern to Malinowski. He
states that theorists do not know where law resides in primitive society. Further there is a
wide range of phenomena which must be classed as
legal and a body of principles to control these
phenomena. Primitive societies with the exception
of some African monarchies contain none of the
legal institutions found in highly developed societies (i.e., codes of law and juridical institutions such as legislative bodies, courts, and
police). The forces of law in primitive society
reside in every basic role relationship (i.e.,
chief-subject); in the reciprocity and mutuality
within societal institutions; and in institutional
interrelationships.[38]

A. R. Radcliffe-Brown

In his essay, "Primitive Law" that appeared
in the Encyclopedia of the Social Sciences
Radcliffe-Brown defines law as social control
through the systematic application of the force of
politically organized society (i.e., organized
legal sanctions). Thus he accepts the definition
of law proposed by Pound. The obligations imposed
on individuals in societies where there are no
legal sanctions are custom, not law. Thus some
traditional societies have no law although all
have customs supported by sanctions.[39]

There is confusion in the attempt to apply
the distinction between criminal and civil law to
preliterate society according to Radcliffe-Brown.
He advocates making a distinction between what he
calls the law of public and private delict. A

public delict is a deed which leads to an organized and regular response on the part of the community or its representatives toward the offender in the form of prescribed punishment (i.e., penal sanction). According to this definition few acts are public delicts in private societies (i.e., incest, sorcery, tribal custom breaches, and sacrilege). A private delict is an action which is subject to a restitutive sanction. Thus private delicts correspond to civil law of modern society with certain differences and are procedures used for avoiding or relieving social conflicts within a community. Private delicts in preliterate societies comprise killing, wounding, adultery, and failure to pay debts. The modern criminal and civil law are derived from the law of public and private delicts.[40]

The law has multiple origins and its initial development is bound up with magic and religion. A wrong committed by a member of a community in the earliest stage of legal evolution may be subject to three sanctions. These are general or diffuse moral, ritual, and penal. On the other hand, an action which constitutes an infringement of individual or group rights may led to the implementation of the retaliatory sanction (i.e., warfare and organized and regulated vengeance).[41]

The next step in the evolution toward formation of a legal system according to Radcliffe-Brown is where definite arbitrators or judges bear evidence, decide responsibility, and assess damages on a voluntary basis since no authority with powers to enforce judgments exists. Finally societies that have centralized political authority (i.e., certain African kingdoms) administer both kinds of law, that is the central authority deals with public delicts and a judicial tribunal deals with private delicts.[42]

Huntington Cairns

Cairns in his book, Law and the Social
Sciences reviews the early history of the relationship of law and anthropology. He notes the contributions of Post, Kohler, and Maine. In particular
Malinowski is singled out for his statements on the
importance of the relationship of law and anthropology and for the development of the functional
approach to the subject. There are three conclusions reached by anthropological theorists that
have a bearing on jurisprudence. These are the
nature of the law, the relationship of legal history
and anthropology, and law and anthropology in
action.[43]

An attempt to define law and apply the definition to primitive society utilizing both Cardozo's
and Malinowski's definitions is made by Cairns.
Cardozo's definition does not apply to primitive
cultures and Malinowski's to advanced cultures.
Since neither definition applies to all cultures,
law in primitive society must be different from
law in modern society. But Cairns states that law
in primitive society must fulfill the same function
as law in advanced society. The conclusion reached
by Cairns is that lack of data about traditional
cultures and the problem of linguistics account for
this problem.[44]

An understanding of the basic ideas underlying
property and the family reveal the true relationship between law and anthropology according to
Cairns. Anthropologists have shown that some
notion of property exists in all cultures. Legal
concepts of property evolve as society moves from
the simple stage of development to the complex.
The hypothesis of primitive cultures possessing
embryonic ideas of the property concept is not
confined to legal theorists but is also believed
by Maine, Morgan, Spencer, and Lowie. The old idea

that only advanced legal systems could deal with
the concept of corporeal property as well as incorporeal property has been dispelled by anthropological theorists. All cultures recognize this
property distinction.[45]

Inheritance and testamentary disposition have
multiple origins. There are a multitude of both
forms of inheritance and family which are interrelated according to Cairns. He feels the family
is primarily a juridic institution. The institution of marriage occupies a central place in all
legal systems and is invested with juridic attributes. Finally anthropology of law supplies comparative data for more accurate legal analysis; it
forms the basis for this history of legal institutions; it enhances the understanding of legal
concepts; and it provides law with a holistic perspective.[46]

E. Adamson Hoebel

In his article, "Law and Anthropology" Hoebel
examines the lack of integration between law and
anthropology. This is due to a misconception of
the nature of law and a failure to attack real
jurisprudence problems. Early anthropological
theorists state there is no law in traditional
society, that custom accounts for everything, or
law is custom. The German school of ethnological
jurisprudence (i.e., Kohler and Post) devised a
system of legal evolution which did not deal with
either the juridical process or the functions of
legal interrelations. The anthropology of law
studies carried out by the Dutch in Indonesia were
not concerned with the theory of law as a social
science. Malinowski was the first anthropologist
to study legal doctrine in terms of behavior.[47]

Hoebel is concerned with the kinds of behavior constituting law and with the characteristics of law. He defines law as a specialized machinery of social control. Most primitive law is not legislated but traditional courts do exist in the form of a tribal council or some similar association. Thus the formal concept of a court is not necessary for the determination of law in a traditional society. The legitimate use of physical coercion is what is necessary for this determination according to Hoebel. The essentials of legal coercion consist of the acceptance by the societal population of the application of physical power by a privileged party for a legitimate cause in a legitimate way at a legitimate time. This comprises the legal sanction. Thus one who is recognized as rightly exerting the element of physical coercion represents the legal in primitive society.[48]

The claimant and defendant shape the law as they play crucial roles in deciding any trouble-case for they lay the grounds of claim, counter-claim, or denial of charges. Thus judgment rendered in any dispute is secondary to the roles of claimant and defendant.[49]

The Hohfeldian system of legal analysis is of use to legal anthropologists according to Hoebel. This system is an aid in four ways: (1) all legal relations are those between particular persons; (2) it clarifies the meaning and content of basic elements in legal relations through definition and functional operations demonstrations; (3) primitive legal relations components are identical with those found in modern societies; and (4) the system can be applied to any social complex of imperative reciprocal relations.[50]

In his book, The Law of Primitive Man Hoebel states that all systems of law have some essential elements in common. Law consists of a specially

demarked set of social norms that are maintained
through the application of sanctions. The entire
operating system of sanctioning norms constitutes
a system of social control. Law as a process is
an aspect of the social control system within
society. A chief function of law is selecting
norms for legal support that are in accord with
the basic social postulates of the culture in
which the law system is set.[51]

Creation of an acceptable definition is difficult due to parochialism and the fact that law
is just part of the social system, often not sep-
arable from other forms of social action. A new
conception as to the nature of law is needed.
Hoebel examines the legal definitions of Cardozo
and Radcliffe-Brown before preceding to formulate
his own definition. He defines law as a social
norm which is legal if its neglect or infraction
is regularly met in threat or in fact by the application of physical force by an individual or group
possessing the socially recognized privilege of
so acting.[52]

The Hohfeldian system of legal analysis is
utilized by Hoebel as the basis for examining the
law as found in traditional society. The fundamental premise of Hohfeld is that all legal relations are between people. Thus a legal issue is
one that concerns the relations between two or
more persons with respect to a thing; every legal
relation is bilateral; and these relations can be
analyzed as fundamental reciprocal relations (i.e.,
demand-right/duty; privilege-right/no demand right;
power/liability; and immunity/no power relation).[53]

In traditional societies, law and custom may
appear to be the same but they are different (i.e.,
according to Hohfeldian doctrine a demand-right
not acted upon by one party engenders a privilege-
right by the plaintiff in primitive system private

law whereas a demand-right not acted upon by defendant in our society causes a further demand-
right of plaintiff). Law is distinguished from
custom in that it endows certain selected individuals with the privilege-right of applying the
sanction of physical coercion if need be according
to Hoebel.[54]

The object in property law is of less significance than the network of legal relations which
determine and prescribe permissible behavior with
respect to that object according to the Hohfeldian
view. An object does not become property until
members of society agree to bestow the property
attribute upon the object by regulating their behavior with respect to the object in a self-limit-
ing manner.[55]

An anthropological approach to property as a
social institution helps clarify inheritance as we
see it as a transference of status from the de-
ceased to his successor. Thus transmission of
property is transmission of status. The contention
that the concept of incorporeal property exists in
traditional society is supported by Hoebel using
Hohfeld's conceptual framework.[56]

Law performs certain functions essential to
the maintenance of most societies. The first
function defines the relationship among societal
members and asserts what activities are permitted
and what are ruled out so as to maintain integration between individual activities and group activities within society. The law's important
contribution to the basic organization of society
is that the law specifically and explicitly defines relations. The second function of law is
the allocation of authority, and the determination
of who may exercise physical coercion as a socially recognized privilege-right, along with the
selection of the most effective forms of physical

sanction to achieve the social ends that the law
serves. Authority is a shifting, temporary thing
in primitive law, and only in a limited number of
situations is it exercised directly by the community.[57]

The third function is the disposition of
trouble cases as they arise. In primitive society
the individual case always holds the threat of
civil strife if procedure breaks down since kin
group is pitted against kin group. The fourth
function is redefining relations between individuals and groups as life conditions change. The
law must decide what principles shall be applied
to conflicts of claims created by culture contact
and change.[58]

The problem of reorienting conduct and re-
directing it through the law when new issues emerge
is called juristic method which is the method of
getting law-jobs done coupled with legal change
accomplished with a minimum of social conflict.
Juristic method is found universally in all societies. It may be the quality of a chief or tribal
council or an institutional quality of a complex
legal system.[59]

The very fact that the bulk of the substance
and procedure of primitive law emerges through case
action tends to keep legal behavior close to the
prevailing social values. Thus primitive society
does not have to rely too heavily on the subterfuge
of legal fiction to achieve legal change.[60]

The effect of magico-religious forces as being
superior to men is of variable influence on primitive legal and social systems according to Hoebel.
It is strongest among peoples whose religion emphasizes the role of ancestral spirits as the law
treats such infractions as crimes.[61]

All legal systems legally prohibit homicide, support the principles of relative exclusiveness in mutual rights, assume the importance of the kinship group, support the kinship group as a medium of property right inheritance, and give cognizance to the existance of rights to private property in some goods. Land is legally treated as belonging to the tribe or kinship group, rarely is it legally treated as an object of private property in traditional societies.[62]

The evolution of law has not been linear according to Hoebel. We do not know for certain what specific laws evolved at any given time for any early society although some of the main lines in the trend of legal forms can be sketched over time. The most simple societies (i.e., simple hunters and gatherers) have little need for law because their societal homogeneity is condusive to orderliness. A distinct effort is made to regularize and resolve disputes and conflicts collectively where the only social controls are communally initiated. Rudimentary law-ways exist (i.e., theft demand damages) but no procedural forms have developed.[63]

The highly organized hunters possess greater variation in forms of legal procedures than their predessors although kinship continues to be of great importance in the law. The law of persons is still the bulkiest part of the legal system. Damages are utilized since economic goods are more readily available and can be equated with physical and mental hurt. Criminal law development is still weak.[64]

Law becomes elaborate with the expansion of gardening-based societies. The effort to establish the interests of the society as a whole as superior to the interests of the kinship group is the main advance of law in this type society. The

substantive law becomes more diversified and the
legal unit shifts from family to the clan. Allocation of rights, duties, privileges, powers, and
immunities with respect to real estate is important. The law of things rivals the law of persons.
Action for damages is universally followed by
physical sanctions if payment is refused or not
possible on the defendant's part.[65]

The emergence of the institutionalized chief-
tainship with retention of the council makes subordinate kingroup private law to community oriented
public law. The chief's law with council backing
becomes public law. Thus the growth of centralized
law whether king or council usually leads to the
further evolution of society.[66]

Hoebel states that the trend of the law is one
of increasing growth and complexity and also one in
which the tendency is to shift the privilege-right
of prosecution and imposition of legal sanctions
from the individual and his kinship group over to
clearly defined public officials representing the
society as such. Thus the judicial function of
public officials steadily wins out over the legal
position of the kinship group. Therefore the significant shift in the development of primitive law
is the shift of emphasis in legal procedure, not
the substantive shift from status to contract.[67]

Paul J. Bohannon

Bohannon in his essay, "Anthropology and the
Law" states that anthropologists want to understand
the way in which a society's law works to uphold
its basic values and to change them; are concerned
with the ways that the law maintains social institutions; with the way in which breaches of law are
defined and resolved in relation to the rest of
the cultural ideals of society; and must discover

the ideal and real levels of the law as people
actually see it.[68]

Laws are not social acts but precepts in terms
of which people are supposed to act. There must be
a social act which people regard as a wrong way to
behave which will undermine societal institutions
for a legal situation to exist. Once a person
oversteps the accepted permissible range of deviation, a counteraction takes place so that the
breach of standards can be corrected. Bohannon
deals primarily with examples of the criminal law
to illustrate his theoretical points.[69]

There are many kinds of what Bohannon calls
counteracting institutions in society such as
courts, lawyers, and police systems. Self-help is
a universal counteracting institution since within
defined limits a wronged person has societal permission to bring about the correction of the situation by which he was wronged. The game solution
which defines for people the range of rules whereby life is largely played is another type of
counteracting institution while the town meeting
also serves as a form of counteraction.[70]

A successful counteraction is followed by a
series of acts called the correction by Bohannon.
Deviant acts can be corrected by making the person
who committed the original wrong carry out the
action in terms of the norm he violated or by
implying some sort of penalty.[71]

In his article, "The Differing Realms of the
Law", Bohannon shows through an analysis of several
studies how difficult it is to delimit the subject
matter of law. He quotes from the works of such
theorists as Hart, Stone, Pospisil, and
Kantorowicz to illustrate the characteristics and
attributes of law in order to better understand
the legal concept.[72]

Law must be distinguished from traditions and fashions. More specifically it must be differentiated from social norm and from custom according to Bohannon. Law is specifically recreated by agents of society in a narrower and recognizable context than custom. Law includes custom but it must also consist of rules capable of reinterpretation by one of society's legal institutions so that the conflicts within nonlegal institutions can be adjusted by legal authority. A distinction can be made between law and custom. Reciprocity is the basis of custom. All institutions including the legal one develop customs. Some customs are restated (i.e., reinstitutionalized) for the more precise purposes of legal institutions. A custom that has been restated in order to make it amenable to the activities of the legal institutions is therefore law. Law is never a reflection of custom.[73]

A legal institution in society allows people to settle their disputes and also it counteracts any abuses of the rules of other societal institutions. Legal institutions face the tasks of (1) disengaging institutions from difficulties and engaging the difficulties within the legal institutional processes; (2) handling trouble-cases within the legal institutional framework; and (3) reengaging trouble-case solutions within the processes of the institution where all the trouble began. There are two aspects of legal institutions that are not shared with other societal institutions. These are the regularized ways of interference in the dysfunctioning non-legal institutions in order to disengage the trouble-case; and the types of rules utilized by the legal institutions (i.e., procedural and substantive).[74]

Bohannon defines law as a body of binding obligations regarded as right by one party and acknowledged as a duty by the other which has been

reinstitutionalized within the legal institution
so that society can continue to function in an
orderly manner on the basis of rules so maintained.[75]

Legal rights are those rights that attach to
norms that have been reinstitutionalized. Thus a
legal right is the restatement of some but never
all of the recognized claims of the persons within
societal institutions made for the purpose of maintaining peaceful and just operations of societal
institutions.[76]

A hypothetical legal realm is devised by
Bohannon based on the assumptions that there is a
power or state present whether sovereign or court;
and only one legal culture is subscribed to by a
people of any given society. This legal realm
consists of municipal systems of law, colonial law,
law in stateless societies, and international law.
These four systems are controlled by "legal cultures" and power systems which are either unicentric or multicentric.[77]

Municipal systems deal with a single legal
culture within a unicentric power system. Colonial
law is characterized by a unicentric power system
with two legal cultures. The mark of the stateless
society is the absence of a unicentric power system and the presence of a bicentric power system
where both units (i.e., lineages) possess approximately equal power. International law is characterized by the presence of a multicentric power
system and two or more legal cultures. There are
many potential and actual problems for a system of
law characterized by both a multicentric power
system and multicultural legal system according
to Bohannon.[78]

Laura Nader

Nader in an article, "The Anthropological Study of Law" reviews the growth of anthropology of law from Maine to Hoebel, noting that these theorists are very descriptive and use the case method for the most part. The major concern for anthropological theorists in the 1920's and '30's was the debate as to whether all societies pos- sessed law. On one side was Radcliffe-Brown and his followers who stated that many traditional societies possessed no law, and on the other side was Malinowski and his followers who stated that all societies possessed law. This debate was followed by the attempt to distinguish between law and custom which added further confusion to the resolution of the problem. Theorists today are no longer concerned with this debate since most accept no single definition of law (i.e., Radcliffe-Brown's or Malinowski's).[79]

A working definition of law is stated by Nader as all societies have rules governing behavior; some rules are preferential and others are pre- scribed by society. In some situations, when a prescribed rule is violated, society will have delegated and agreed upon ways of punishing the violator(s). The functions of law are to create conformity with norms, to settle disputes, and to create conflicts.[80]

Some of the research on the subject of uni- versal characteristics of law are reviewed by Nader as found in the writings of Maine, Malinowski, Hoebel, and Pospisil. Maine's three stages (i.e., law by Themistes, customary law, and the code of law) are the earliest attempt to state universals while Malinowski is the first theorist in the twentieth century to deal with law universals. Hoebel deals with legal universals by referring to the Hohfeldian reciprocal relationships while

Pospisil states his four universal attributes of
law. Nader feels that these universal characteristics are really empirical generalizations, and
little work has been directed toward explaining
these generalizations with the exception of
Malinowski. Reference is made to Maine's general-
ization about societal movement from status to
contract and to Durkheim's postulate concerning
the shift from repressive law to restitutive law
as society evolved from traditional to modern in
technology.[81]

Nader traces the history of the idea that
there are as many frameworks of law as there are
types of groups. Durkheim (i.e., the effect of
repressive or restitutive sanctions on organic or
mechanical solidarity type societies), Maine
(i.e., tort and crime and their relation to kin
organized versus territorially organized society),
and Hoebel (i.e., typology of procedures used in
law settlement) are presented as illustrations of
this point.[82]

Functionalism as a descriptive approach (i.e.,
Maine, de Coulange, Bachofen, McLennen, Frazer,
and Durkheim), the interrelation of law and economics (i.e., Marx, Weber, and Hoebel), and the interrelation of law and politics (i.e., Nadel) are all
discussed by Nader. The methodology used to
describe particular legal systems is explored
through the works of Llewellyn, Hoebel, and
Bohannon. Social change and the law is discussed
in terms of the evolution and development of
particular legal systems through analysis of the
writings of Maine and Hoebel.[83]

A critique of the field of legal anthropology
is presented by Nader. She states that the recent
trend has been descriptive, functional analyses
of law systems, both in isolated and culture contact situations. The tendency has been to treat

the legal system as an institution virtually
isolated and independent from other societal institutions outside the social control context. It is
difficult to compare total legal systems if one
uses the models presented by Hoebel or Bohannon
according to Nader. Several questions are raised
which deal with societal law remedy agents or
agencies by Nader. She also analyzes the dispute
case which is considered a societal universal by
most anthropological theorists.[84]

Several assumptions made by Nader concerning
anthropology and the law such as the practical
number of disputes allowed in any particular society; the number of formal procedures that are used
by any one society to prevent and/or settle griev-
ances; and the number and mode of choices present
in a society to settle disputes.[85]

J. A. Barnes

Barnes in his essay, "Law As Politically
Active: An Anthropological View" notes that the
history of legal anthropology has been slow to
develop as many early theorists have been content
with the analyses put forth by Maine and
Malinowski. Only after the Malinowski--Radcliffe-
Brown dispute, which made evolutionary schemes
unfashionable coupled with a movement away from
substantive law analysis to law in action study,
did the legal institution have an opportunity to
influence anthropological theorists. Barnes is
concerned with an analysis of government and law
as seen in practical situations. He examines jural
machinery in stateless societies, law in plural
societies, and the effects of politician/adminis-
trators on the legal apparatus of society.[86]

Many primitive societies are stateless since
power is diffuse rather than concentrated.

Stateless societies lack courts with power to enforce judgments. Alliances of groups of approximately equal power secure orderly existence. In plural societies, peoples of differing ways of life may have different expectations about what is right and wrong yet have to live alongside one another. The important characteristic of the plural societal type is the fact that one segment of society imposes or attempts to impose its norms on the other segment who do not accept these norms but are coerced into partial conformity.[87]

An example of a legal apparatus operated by politicians who are also administrators is illustrated by Barnes. The society analyzed has a legal system run by men who are simultaneously politicians and executives as well as judges and police. This type of legal system has limited power since it cannot readily enforce its judgments according to Barnes.[88]

Leopold Pospisil

Pospisil in his essay, "Law and Order" states that early anthropologists regarded primitive societies as being regulated by custom with group consensus settling all disputes. These theorists concluded that an absence of law was a special characteristic of primitive society (i.e., theories of Hartland, W. H. R. Rivers, and Durkheim). As a reaction to this trend (i.e., law as custom or norms of behavior which is a static concept) developed, there emerged a school of theorists under Radcliffe-Brown who defined law so narrowly that the concept could not be applied to many primitive societies. In reaction to this second group of anthropological theorists, a third trend emerged characterized by the thinking of Bohannon and his followers. These theorists have attempted to comprehend legal phenomena through the verstehen

tradition of Weber applied to the legal structure
and content of a particular traditional society.
No analytical definition of law is offered by this
group of theorists, only working definitions.[89]

In reaction to these three schools of legal
anthropology, Pospisil proposes to define law and
deal with the legal institution in ninety-five
traditional societies. He proposes to examine the
form in which legal phenomena are manifested in
these societies. Pospisil examines three possi-
bilities of conceiving law forms or manifestations
adapted from Llewellyn and Hoebel. These are (1)
through abstract rules that either form the content
of legal codifications in literate societies or a
set of verbalized ideals in the minds of knowl-
edgeable individuals in nonliterate society; (2)
actual behavior of societal members; and (3) principles abstracted from decisions of legal authorities in settling disputes.[90]

These three frameworks are used by Pospisil
to examine the field of legal anthropology. Abstract rules that have been embodied within the
coded law of society or in the memory of preliterate peoples as the proper and exclusive manifestation of law represents the major legal tradition in Western Europe. The long emphasis on
abstract rules in the legal sphere has resulted in
a jurisprudence called legalism. This philosophy
of law states that the individual legal rules themselves, not the parties to disputes are seen as
the exclusive and concrete solutions for particular
disputes. Pospisil states that the virtual lack of
rules in many traditional societies places them
without law, and the legal concept would cease to
be universal according to legalism. Even in societies possessing abstract rules, the conception
of law as a body of abstract rules is untenable
according to Pospisil. Thus the sole existence of
abstract legal rules in a society

does not constitute by itself evidence that these
rules in themselves exercise social control over
members of society. Pospisil presents several
other arguments against the legal concept as
abstract rules.[91]

Rules and principles of law abstracted from
the actual behavior of a people present a number
of difficulties which Pospisil elaborates upon.
First there is the problem of behavioral variabil-
ity; second one cannot equate law with behavior
patterns; and third law often differs from actual
behavior.[92]

Pospisil investigates the hypothesis that
legal decisions offer the best way to investigate
law (i.e., principles abstracted from judicial
decisions). He examines the writings of Holmes,
Hoebel, Llewellyn, Gluckman, as well as his own
data. Pospisil concludes that this third possibility of conceiving law forms is correct and lists
seven reasons for his conclusion.[93]

The term law is applied to a construct of the
human mind for the sake of convenience. Phenomena
of social control often represent a continuum
rather than qualitative clusters with clearly defined gaps between them. Anthropological theorists
according to Pospisil define law as _ius_ or law
proper, not as _lex_, law as an abstract tool. Most
nonliterate and some literate but non-European
societies do not view law as a formalistic act by
a formally instituted authority pronouncing a
formal verdict which is then physically enforced.[94]

The conclusion is reached by Pospisil that law
(ius) manifests itself in the form of a decision
passed by a legal authority by which a dispute is
solved, or a party is advised before any legally
relevant behavior takes place, or by which approval
is given to a previous solution of a dispute made

by the participants before it is brought to the
attention of the authority. Law has two aspects:
a decision serves not only to resolve a dispute
but it also represents a precedent and an ideal 95
for those who are not party to that controversy.

Notes to Chapter IV

1 Henry Sumner Maine, Ancient Law, Boston:
Beacon Press, 1956, pgs. 109-119.

2 Ibid., 120-139.

3 Ibid., 140-156.

4 Ibid., 157-165.

5 William Graham Sumner, Folkways, Boston:
Ginn and Company, 1906, pgs. 48-49.

6 Ibid., 50.

7 Ibid., 53-57.

8 Robert H. Lowie, Primitive Law, New York:
Harper Torchbook, 1961, pgs. 397-406.

9 Ibid., 407-416.

10 Ibid., 417-425.

11 Robert H. Lowie, Anthropology and Law, In
The Social Sciences and Their Interrelations,
W.F. Ogburn & A. Goldenweiser (eds.), Boston:
Houghton Mifflin Company, 1927, pgs. 50-54.

12 Ibid., 55-57.

13 Arthur S. Diamond, Primitive Law, London:
Watts & Company, 1935, pgs. 1-55.

14 Ibid., 56-78.

15 Ibid., 79-100.

16 Ibid., 101-150.

17 Ibid., 151-201.

18 Ibid., 202-247.

19 Ibid., 248-285.

20 Ibid., 286-301.

21 Ibid., 302-329.

22 Arthur S. Diamond, The Evolution of Law and Order, Connecticut: Greenwood Press, 1951, pgs. 44-49.

23 Ibid., 50-56.

24 Ibid., 137-146.

25 Ibid., 147-168.

26 Ibid., 169-198.

27 Ibid., 275-279.

28 Ibid., 280-287.

29 Bronislaw Malinowski, Crime and Custom in Savage Society, New York: Harcourt Brace and Company, 1926, pgs. 2-5.

30 Ibid., 55-59.

31 Ibid., 63-68, 72-83.

32 Bronislaw Malinowski, Introduction, In Law and Order in Polynesia, H.I. Hogbin, Connecticut: The Shoe String Press, 1961, pgs. xix-xx.

33 Ibid., xxi-xxvii.

34 Ibid., xxviii-xl.

35 Ibid., xli-li.

36 Ibid., lii-lx.

37 Ibid., lxi-lxvi.

38 Ibid., lxvii-lxxi.

39 A.R. Radcliffe-Brown, Primitive Law, Encyclopedia of the Social Sciences, E. Seligman and A. Johnson (eds.), New York: Macmillan Company, 1933, pgs. 202-203.

40 Ibid., 204.

41 Ibid., 205.

42 Ibid., 206.

143

43 Huntington Cairns, Law and the Social Sciences, New York: Harcourt Brace and Company, 1935, pgs. 7–15.

44 Ibid., 16–23.

45 Ibid., 24–33.

46 Ibid., 34–45.

47 E. Adamson Hoebel, Law and Anthropology, Virginia Law Review, 32, (1946), pgs. 835–840.

48 Ibid., 841–844.

49 Ibid., 845– 849.

50 Ibid., 850–853.

51 E. Adamson Hoebel, The Law of Primitive Man, Cambridge, Massachusetts: Harvard University Press, 1967, pgs. 4–7.

52 Ibid., 8–15.

53 Ibid., 16–20.

54 Ibid., 21–28.

55 Ibid., 46–50.

56 Ibid., 51–53.

57 Ibid., 54–57.

58 Ibid., 58–60.

59 Ibid., 61–63.

60 Ibid., 275–279.

61 Ibid., 280–287.

62 Ibid., 288–295.

63 Ibid., 296–301.

64 Ibid., 302–309.

65 Ibid., 310–316.

66 Ibid., 317–325.

67 Ibid., 326–331.

68 Paul J. Bohannon, Anthropology and the
Law, In Horizons of Anthropology, Saul Tax (ed.),
Chicago: Aldine Publishing Company, 1964, pgs.
191–193.

69 Ibid., 194–196.

70 Ibid., 197–199.

71 Ibid., 197–199.

72 Paul J. Bohannon, The Differing Realms
of the Law, The American Anthropologist, 67, no.
6, part 2 (1965), The Ethnology of Law Special
Supplement, pg. 33.

73 Ibid., 34.

74 Ibid., 35–36.

75 Ibid., 37–38.

76 Ibid., 39.

77 Ibid., 40.

78 Ibid., 41.

79 Laura Nader, The Anthrolopogical Study of
Law, The American Anthropologist, 67, no. 6, part
2 (1965), The Ethnology of Law Special Supplement,
pgs. 3–7.

80 Ibid., 8–12.

81 Ibid., 13–15.

82 Ibid., 16–18.

83 Ibid., 19–21.

84 Ibid., 22–23.

85 Ibid., 24–25.

145

86   J.A. Barnes, Law as Politically Active
Anthropological View, In Studies In The
Sociology of Law, Geoffrey Sawer (ed.)., Canberra:
The Australian National University, 1961, pgs. 167–
171.

87   Ibid., 122–186.

88   Ibid., 187–193.

89   Leopold Pospisil, Law and Order, In
Introduction to Cultural Anthropology, James
Clifton (ed.), Boston: Houghton Mifflin Company,
1968 pgs. 201–203.

90   Ibid., 204.

91   Ibid., 206–209.

92   Ibid., 210–213.

93   Ibid., 214–217.

94   Ibid., 218–219.

95   Ibid., 220–222.

CONCLUSION

Model Building

In 1975 two theorists published their
thoughts of what sociological models of society
should be, based on their interpretations of the
writings of Thomas Kuhn.[1] Both George Ritzer in
his book Sociology: A Multiple Paradigm Science
and Charles Reasons in his article "Social
Thoughts and Social Structure: Competing Paradigms in Criminology" were attempting to bring
order to a subject that has been noted for its
multiplicity of theories.

The Paradigms of Ritzer

According to Ritzer, there are currently only
three basic paradigms in sociology. These are the
social facts paradigm, social definition paradigm,
and social behavior paradigm.[2] A paradigm is
defined as "a fundamental image of the subject
matter within a science. It serves to define what
should be studied, what questions should be asked,
and what rules should be followed in interpreting
the answers obtained. The paradigm is the broad-
est unit of consensus within a science and serves
to differentiate one scientific community or sub-
community from another. It subsumes, defines, and
interrelates the exemplars, theories, and methods/
tools that exist within it."[3]

Criminology and its subdivision, sociology of
law should fit into one or more of these paradigms
if Ritzer is basically correct in his analysis.
In order to accomplish this task, we will begin the
analysis of Ritzer's work by first defining the
various applicable paradigms and describing their
theories. Briefly the social factist is interested
in the development of grand, abstract theory. Institutions, social structures, and social groups

146

are the basic type of facts of interest to adherents of this paradigm.[4]   Social definitions are concerned with debunking myths about society and devote themselves to changing various things that are regarded by them as detrimental to society. Social definitions are basically social interactionists concerning themselves with the relationship between individual and social group.[5]   The social behaviorists accept both the need to develop theory and use sophisticated quantitative methods of analysis.   The adherents to the social behavior paradigm concentrate on the individual.[6]

Social Facts Paradigm

The social facts paradigm is composed of two theories, structural-functionalism and conflict theory.   Structural-functionalists feel that structures and institutions can contribute to the maintenance of other social facts and can also have negative consequences for them (i.e., utilize the concepts of function and dysfunction).   followers of this theory justify the status quo and tend to have a conservative societal orientation (i.e., emphasize order in society and de-emphasize conflict and change).[7]   In particular structural-functionalists are oriented toward the analysis of social structures and institutions.   Concern is with relationships between structures, between institutions, and between structures and institutions.   The individual is largely controlled by social facts that are external and coercive. Functionalists view society as static or in a state of moving equilibrium.   They strongly emphasize the fact that society is orderly; that every societal element contributes to stability; and that society is kept together informally by norms, values, and common morality.[8]

Conflict theory for the most part is simply a series of positions directly antithetical to

structural-functionalist ideas according to
Ritzer. Thus conflict theorists are oriented toward the study of social structures and institutions like functionalists but perceive society as
based on conflict and consensus emphasizing the
role of power in maintaining societal order.[9] In
particular conflict theorists see every structure
and institution of society subject to change,
conflict ridden, and riddled by dissension. Whatever order there is in society stems from the
coercion of the powerless by those in authority.
Differential authority is an attribute of various
societal positions. Authority does not reside in
individuals but in these positions. Thus the
individual is concerned with societal positions
and the differential distribution of power among
these positions. Hence the structural origin of
conflicts must be sought in the arrangement of
social roles endowed with expectations of domination or subjection (i.e., authority implies both
superordination and subordination). Finally, the
identification of various authority roles within
society is the primary focus of conflict theorists.[10]

Both theories of the social facts paradigm
tend to be holistic (i.e., look at society as
composed of interrelated parts with an interest in
the interrelationship between the parts); both
theories ignore each other (i.e., one emphasizes
societal integration while the other emphasizes
societal conflict); both share an evolutionary
view of social change; and both are basically
equilibrium theories.[11]

Social Definition Paradigm

The social definition paradigm is composed of
three theories, action, symbolic interactionism,
and phenomenology. Action theorists (ala Weber)
view the individual as possessing a dynamic,

creative, voluntaristic mind. They see Weber's
verstehen concept as a method for gathering data
on social institutions and social structures, not
as a method for understanding the mental process.
The action theorist attempts to put himself in
the place of the actor, not in order to comprehend
the person but to understand the cultural and
societal milieu in which the actor exists.[12]
Social action theorists examine the problem-solv-
ing process through the minds of the actor under
study. They examine the actor's means to ends
whether both are valued in the same manner or
differently utilizing the "verstehen" concept (i.e.,
empathy and reliving the experiences of the actor).
The feelings, emotions, and habits of the actor
are sometimes receptive to analysis using this
concept (i.e., interpretive understanding).[13]

Symbolic interactionism theory deals with
covert aspects of behavior. Theorists view behavior as a process of interpretation inserted be-
ween the environmental stimulus and response of
the actor. Social facts are not viewed as things
controlling or coercing the individual but only
as the framework within which symbolic interaction
takes place. Individuals fit their actions to
those of others through a process of interpretation.
Through this process actors form groups, the action
of the group serving as the action of all actors
within it. The world of the actor is found in the
process of interpretation or orientation of himself
vis-a-vis the group. The mind is a process in
which the individual interacts with himself and
others through symbol utilization.[14]

Phenomenological theory is more philosophical
than sociological. These theorists state that man
constitutes and reconstitutes what is real (i.e.,
objective social reality is not independent of the
individual). Thus to define a situation as real
makes it real. Phenomenologists try to comprehend

the meaning that the actor's behavior has for him by both studying the process through which social facts are created by the actor rather than the social facts themselves and by examining the ongoing process of reality construction in society as social facts do not possess an objective existence. By uncovering the processes through which social order emerges from the negotiative behaviors of everyday life, phenomenologists hope to learn how people engage in the process of creating the social facts that are coercive on them. Order and meaning cannot have an objective existence since people impose order and meaning on themselves through manipulation and molding of norms. Reality is what one makes of it. Thus order and social reality have a tenuous existence according to this theory.[15]

Social Behavior Paradigm

Sociology of criminal law theorists tend not to be oriented toward the social behavior paradigm by definition if one goes according to Sutherland. He states that this division of criminology "is an attempt at systematic analysis of the conditions under which criminal laws develop."[16] The crime causation and crime control divisions of criminology appear to be primarily concerned with the social behaviorist paradigm as they tend to be individual oriented. On the other hand, sociology of criminal law is theoretically both group and individual-group oriented since it deals with people on the basis of laws and legal institutions, not on the basis of individual behavior patterns. Thus sociology of criminal law theorists would tend to either fit into the social facts or social definition paradigms. Therefore one will not deal with the theories of the social behavior paradigm in this paper (see Ritzer, Sociology: A Multiple

Paradigm Science, Allyn & Bacon, 1975, Chapter 4,
pgs. 145-177).

The Paradigms of Reasons

Reasons creates what he calls three major
paradigms for the field of criminology. The
kinds of people paradigm asserts that the causes
of criminality is in the characteristics of the
criminal (i.e., positivistic view).[17] The kinds
of environments paradigm asserts that crime is a
product of the social system (i.e., social deter-
ministic view).[18] Both these paradigms accept a
legalistic definition of crime (i.e., behavior
violating criminal laws) according to Reasons.[19]
The third paradigm, power/conflict recognizes the
importance of power, politics, and people in
creating, sustaining, and shaping conditions conducive to criminality.[20]

The three paradigms proposed by Reasons "fit"
into the three paradigms proposed by Ritzer which
has been expounded upon in a previous section of
this essay. Reasons' kind of people paradigm can
be placed in part in both the social behavior and
social definition paradigms. His kinds of environments and power/conflict paradigms can both be
placed in the social facts paradigm. It is possible that if Reasons knew of the work of Ritzer
before creating his paradigms he would have utilized the concise system devised by the latter
rather than the vague descriptions he uses that in
actuality overlap with two of Ritzer's paradigms
or are part of the same paradigm.

Sociology of law theorists should look at
behavior patterns which violate other norms which
transcend the political state (i.e., basic concepts
of humanity and justice) rather than a continuation
of analyzing those behaviors which are officially
prohibited by state laws according to Reasons.[21]

To comprehend the law, power/conflict theorists want to demystify the misconceptions concerning the nature and function of the law. The
law must be understood in the context of power,
politics, and people.[22] Legal system personnel
hold values, attitudes, and orientations which
influence their professional actions preventing
them from operating in a value-free intellectual
atmosphere. The law is an instrument of those in
power who use it to maintain their positions of
high status and privilege in society through
utilization of interest groups whose function is
to put pressure on legal system personnel.[23]

The power/conflict paradigm demystifies the
traditional conception of the criminal and non-
criminal which pervades contemporary criminological thought. By focusing on the political nature
of criminal definitions, their application, and
enforcement - the power/conflict perspective
asserts that crime is a product of current power
differentials and conflicting world views. Crime
is a definition of behavior made by officials of
the state and is not inherent in an act. Those
behaviors which are offensive to the establishment
will be made crimes. Rather than focusing on the
crimes of the common criminal, this paradigm places
emphasis on the lawless behavior of the state and
those in power positions. When attending to common
crimes and criminals, paradigmatic emphasis is
placed on the oppressive, arbitrary, and self-
serving nature of the criminal justice system and
its injustices from the offender's perspective.[24]

Paradigms Applied to the Sociology of Law

In a series of four articles Robert Rich sub-
jected the writings of several major theorists in
the sociology of law field to analysis utilizing
the paradigmatic perspective proposed by Ritzer.[25]

The results of this research revealed some interesting findings. The major finding of this research is that most theorists have been and are adherents of structural-functional theory (i.e., consensus theory).

In the area of sociology of civil law both classical (Ehrlich, Weber, Timasheff, and Gurvitch) and contemporary theorists (Evan, Davis, Parsons, Aubert, Selznick, Skolnick, Sawer, Schur, and Akers) are structural-functionalists. Only Renner is a conflict theorist. The same findings apply to sociological jurisprudence. All theorists whether classical (Pound and Cardozo) or contemporary (Llewellyn, Stone, Hall, Allen, Fuller, and Hart) are structural-functionalists. Anthropology of law theorists show the same theoretical bias. Maine, Sumner, Malinowski, Radcliffe-Brown, Lowie, and Diamond of the classical period and Hoebel, Bohannon, Nader, and Pospisil of the contemporary period are all structural-functionalists.

Only when dealing with sociology of criminal law theorists does one find a mix of theoretical positions. Beccaria, Bentham, and Tarde are social interactionists while Durkheim is a structural-functionalist. The contemporary theorists are either structural-functionalists or conflict theorists. Jeffery, Schur, Gibbs, and Akers are adherents to the consensus view while Turk, Hills, Chambliss, Quinney, and Reasons are adherents to the conflict view.

It can be concluded that most sociology of law theorists are adherents to structural-functionalist theory, some to conflict theory, and a few adhere to symbolic interactionist theory. Thus according to the Ritzer paradigmatic scheme, most theorists would fall within the social facts paradigm. The majority of sociology of law theorists would probably agree that law is a social norm and a form of social control. Thus all view man as manipulated by normative systems (i.e., value-attitudes) and social control agencies. Finally the source of control over the individual would be for the most part societal social structures and institutions that would be coercive in nature.

Future of Sociology of Law

Sociology of law has come a long way in terms of theory building since the late Nineteenth Century. A brief examination of key publications will enable us to determine the contemporary state of the art.

Status of Research

The best theoretical studies in the author's opinion are limited in number. An examination of the sociology of civil law area reveals the work of Renner (1904), Ehrlich (1913), and Weber (1922) as crucial in the early years with that of Sawer (1961 and 1965), Davis (1962), Evan (1962), Schur (1968), Chambliss and Seidman (1970), and Black (1976) of importance for contemporary theorists. This means that the work of Timasheff (1939) and Gurvitch (1947) have not added to the growth of the field. Further the multiplicity of readers such as Simon (1968), Friedman and Macaulay (1969), Aubert (1969), Schwartz and Skolnick (1970), Sutherland and Werthman (1971), Akers and Hawkins (1975), and Black and Mileski (1976) have not added much to the growth of theory building since much of the material in these readers has been reprinted several times over.

The same type of findings do not apply to sociology of criminal law. Durkheim's contributions in 1893 and 1897 have seen only limited application in American theory until quite recent times. Quinney in a number of books and articles

in the late '60's and '70's along with Chambliss
(1971, 1973, 1975, 1976) have put forth a conflict
perspective. This theoretical view has been supported by Turk (1969), Hills (1971), Reasons
(1974), and Pepinsky (1976). Thus criminal law
theory has made definite advances over the structural-functional approach.

Unfortunately sociological jurisprudence has
somewhat lagged behind in definitive studies.
Pound's articles in 1911-1912 were historical in
nature and it was not until Hall's book of 1952
that the field moved ahead. The work of Hart
(1961), Llewellyn (1962), Allen (1964), Fuller
(1964), and Stone (1966) are in the structural-
functionalist tradition and offer sound material.
The more recent work of Friedman (1967 and 1969),
Black (1972), and Nonet (1976) offer hope for
significant advancements.

Anthropology of law theory is even more limited in definitive studies than the other areas
of sociology of law. The work of Maine (1861 and
1883), Durkheim (1893, 1897, and 1912), and
Malinowski (1926) along with that of Diamond (1935)
made a good start in theory building. Unfortunately one only finds Hoebel filling the gap (1941 and
1954) until recent times. Barnes (1961) and
Bohannon (1964 and 1965) have added to the field
but the works of Nader (1965 and 1969) and Pospisil
(1968) have for the most part been reworkings of
older theoretical perspectives.

Funding

In 1962 the Russell Sage Foundation began
funding programs in law and social science at
selected American universities and in 1964 also
aided the establishment of the Law and Society
Association. In 1966 the Law and Society Review

came into being with Sage Foundation funds. The
same year a summer institute for research in law
and social sciences was established with funds
from Sage and the National Science Foundation.
This program lasted until 1972.[26] Unfortunately
there has been no concerted effort to directly
fund research in the sociology of law area since
1971 with the exception of the Law and Social
Sciences Program of the National Science Foundation. The Law Enforcement Assistance Administration of the Department of Justice has had responsibility for support of research on the criminal
law since 1968 but has funded few such projects.

Journals

There are currently three interdisciplinary
journals published which deal with sociology of
law as a specific topic. These are Law and Society
Review (1966), British Journal of Law and Society
(1974), and Law and Human Behavior (1977). All
major criminology, sociology, as well as law
journals publish articles dealing with sociology
of law from time to time. There appears to be no
major policy concerning the direction that articles
should take but analysis of most publications shows
that articles oriented toward structural functional
theory are most acceptable with some conflict
theory now becoming popular.

American versus European Theory

There appears to be a historical bias in
favor of European theory over American in the
evolution of the sociology of law field until the
1960's. Much of the theory building has been
centered in France, Germany, and England with interest generated in Italy, Portugal, Canada,
Australia, and the Scandinavian countries. Although American theorists have been quite productive

since the early '60's, they have taken the lead
in theoretical orientation from Europeans (i.e.,
accepted conflict and radical perspectives from
English, German, and French theorists).

The author would conclude that the sociology
of law is a viable subdivision of criminology
that has great growth potential in the United
States especially if more departments of sociology
and schools of criminal justice would offer
courses. It would also be extremely useful if
social policy makers would utilize the field for
decision-making and encourage more research in
theory building in future years.

Notes to Conclusion

1 Thomas Kuhn, <u>The Structure of Scientific</u>
<u>Revolutions</u>, 2nd edition, Chicago: University of
Chicago Press, 1970.

2 George Ritzer, <u>Sociology: A Multiple</u>
<u>Paradigm Science</u>, Boston: Allyn and Bacon, 1975,
pg. 24.

3 <u>Ibid.</u>, 189.

4 <u>Ibid.</u>, 24.

5 <u>Ibid.</u>, 24-25.

6 <u>Ibid.</u>, 25.

7 <u>Ibid.</u>, 48-57.

8 George Ritzer, Sociology: A Multiple
Paradigm Science, <u>The American Sociologist</u>, 10
(August, 1975), pgs. 159-160.

9 George Ritzer, <u>Sociology: A Multiple</u>
<u>Paradigm Science</u>, Boston: Allyn and Bacon, 1975,
pgs. 57-67.

10 George Ritzer, Sociology: A Multiple
Paradigm Science, <u>The American Sociologist</u>, 10
(August, 1975), pg. 160.

11 George Ritzer, <u>Sociology: A Multiple</u>
<u>Paradigm Science</u>, Boston: Allyn and Bacon, 1975,
pg. 63.

12 George Ritzer, Sociology: A Multiple
Paradigm Science, <u>The American Sociologist</u>, 10
(August, 1975), pgs. 161-162.

13 George Ritzer, <u>Sociology: A Multiple</u>
Paradigm Science, Boston: Allyn and Bacon, 1975,
pgs. 86-87; George Ritzer, Sociology: A
Multiple Paradigm Science, <u>The American</u>
<u>Sociologist</u>, 10 (August, 1975), pg. 162.

159

14 George Ritzer, Sociology: A Multiple Paradigm Science, Boston: Allyn and Bacon, 1975, pgs. 96-115; George Ritzer, Sociology: A Multiple Paradigm Science. The American Sociologist, 10 (August, 1975), pg. 162.

15 George Ritzer, Sociology: A Multiple Paradigm Science, Boston: Allyn and Bacon, 1975, pgs. 96-115; George Ritzer, Sociology: A Multiple Paradigm Science, The American Sociologist, 10 (August, 1975), pg. 162.

16 E.H. Sutherland and D.R. Cressey, Criminology, Philadelphia: J.B. Lippincott Company, 1970, pg. 3.

17 Charles Reasons, Social Thought and Social Structure: Competing Paradigms in Criminology, Criminology, 13, no. 3, November, 1975, pgs. 336-337.

18 Ibid., 337-339.

19 Ibid., 342.

20 Ibid., 342-343.

21 Ibid., 344.

22 Ibid., 346.

23 Ibid., 346-347.

24 Ibid., 348-349.

25 Robert M. Rich, "The Sociology of Law: Toward a Paradigmatic Perspective" 1976; "The Sociology of Criminal Law: Toward a Paradigmatic Perspective", 1976; "Sociological Jurisprudence: Toward a Paradigmatic Perspective", 1975; and "The Anthropology of Law: Toward a Paradigmatic Perspective", 1975.

26 Jack Ladinsky, The Teaching of Law and Social Science Courses in the United States, Working Paper number 11, Center For Law and Behavioral Science, University of Wisconsin, Madison, Wisconsin, 1974.

Bibliography

I. Sociology of Civil Law

Akers, Ronald and Hawkins, Richard (eds.). Law
    and Control In Society. Englewood Cliffs,
    New Jersey: Prentice-Hall, 1975.

Albrow, Martin. "Legal Positivism and Bourgeois
    Materialism: Max Weber's View of the
    Sociology of Law", British Journal of Law and
    Society II (Summer, 1975), 14-31.

Aubert, Vilhelm. "Researches in the Sociology of
    Law", The American Behavioral Scientist VII,
    no. 4 (1963), 16-17.

_____(ed.). Sociology of Law.
    Baltimore: Penguin Books, 1969.

Auerbach, Carl. "Legal Tasks for the Sociologist",
    Law and Society Review I (November, 1966),
    91-104.

Baxi, Upendra. "Durkheim and Legal Evolution:
    Some Problems of Disproof-Rejoinder", Law
    and Society Review VIII (Summer, 1974),
    645-668.

Black, Donald. The Behavior of Law. New York:
    Academic Press, 1976.

_____ and Mileski, Maureen (eds.). The
    Social Organization of Law. New York:
    Academic Press, 1976.

Bohannon, Paul. "Law and Legal Institutions", in
    International Encyclopedia of the Social
    Sciences. New York: Free Press, 1968.

Brito, M.E. Sociology of Law - A Selected
    Bibliography. Lisbon: Centro de Ciencias
    Politicas e Sociais, 1972.

Cairns, Huntington. Law and the Social Sciences.
    New York: Harcourt, Brace and Company, 1935,
    Pp. 125-167.

160

Chambliss, William and Seidman, Robert.
Sociology of the Law: A Research Bibliography. Berkeley, California: The
Glendessary Press, 1970.

David, Rene and Brierley, John. Major Legal
Systems In the World Today. London: Stevens
and Sons, 1968, Pp. 153-167.

Davis, F. James et al. Society and the Law. New
York: Free Press, 1962.

Ehrlich, Eugen. Fundamental Principles of the
Sociology of Law. Cambridge, Massachusetts:
Harvard University Press, 1936.

_____. "The Sociology of Law", Harvard
Law Review XXXVI, number 2 (December, 1922),
130-144.

Evan, William (ed.). Law and Sociology. New
York: Free Press, 1962.

Freund, Julien. The Sociology of Max Weber.
New York: Random House, 1968.

Friedman, Lawrence and Macaulay, Stuart. Law and
the Behavioral Sciences. Indianapolis:
Bobbs-Merrill, 1969.

Friedman, Lawrence. Society and the Legal System.
New York: Basic Books, Forthcoming.

Gibbs, Jack. "The Sociology of Law and Normative
Phenomena", American Sociological Review
XXXI (June, 1966), 315-325.

Grace, Clive and Wilkinson, Philip. "Social
Action as a Methodology for the Sociology of
Law", British Journal of Law and Society I
(Winter, 1974), 185-194.

Gurvitch, Georges. "Major Problems of the
Sociology of Law", Journal of Social
Philosophy VI, number 3 (April, 1941,),
198-215.

_____. Sociology of Law. London: Routledge and Kegan Paul, 1947.

Herpin, N. Les Sociologues Americians et Le Siecle. Paris: P.U.F., 1973.

McDonald, Lynn. The Sociology of Law and Order. Montreal: Book Center Inc., 1976.

Parsons, Talcott. "The Law and Social Control", in Evan, William (ed.) Law and Society. New York: Free Press, 1962, Pp. 56-72.

Partridge, P.H. "Ehrlich's Sociology of Law", in Sawer, Geoffrey (ed.) Studies in the Sociology of Law. Canberra: The Australian National University, 1961, Pp. 1-26.

Pepinsky, Harold. "Anarchist-Communism as an Alternative to Due Process", paper presented to the American Sociological Association, August, 1976.

Pocar, V. La Sociologia del Diritto Negli anni 60, Saggio Bibliografico. Reggio Calabria: Meridionali, 1975.

Pound, Roscoe. "Sociology of Law", in Gurvitch, Georges and Moore, Wilbert (eds.) Twentieth Century Sociology. New York: The Philosophical Society, 1945, Pp. 297-340.

Renner, Karl. The Institutions of Private Law. London: Routledge and Kegan Paul, 1949.

Rich, Robert M. "The Sociology of Law: oward A Paradigmatic Perspective", paper presented to the American Sociological Association, August, 1976.

Rose, Arnold. "Law and the Cause of Social Problems", Social Problems XVI (Summer, 1968), 33-43.

Sawer, Geoffrey (ed.). Studies in the Sociology of Law. Canberra: The Australian National University, 1961.

163

_____. Law In Society. London: Oxford University Press, 1965.

Schur, Edwin. Law and Society: A Sociological View. New York: Random House, 1968.

Schwartz, Richard and Miller, James. "Legal Evolution and Societal Complexity", American Journal of Sociology LXX (September, 1964), 159-169.

_____ and Skolnick, Jerome (eds.). Society and the Legal Order. New York: Basic Books, 1970.

Selznick, Philip. "The Sociology of Law", in International Encyclopedia of the Social Sciences. New York: Free Press, 1968, Pp. 50-58.

_____. "The Sociology of Law" in Simon, Rita (ed.) The Sociology of Law. Scranton, Pennsylvania: Chandler Publishing Company, 1968, Pp. 190-199.

Simon, Rita. The Sociology of Law. Scranton, Pennsylvania: Chandler Publishing Company, 1968.

Skolnick, Jerome. "The Sociology of Law in America: Overview and Trends", Social Problems XIII, number 1 (Summer, 1965), 4-39.

_____. "Social Research on Legality: A Reply to Auerbach", Law and Society Review I (November, 1966), 105-110.

Stoljar, S.J. "Weber's Sociology of Law", in Sawer, Geoffrey (ed.) Studies in the Sociology of Law. Canberra: The Australian National University, 1961, Pp. 31-52.

Sutherland, Jon and Werthman, Michael (eds.) Comparative Concepts of Law and Order. Glenview, Illinois: Scott, Foresman and Company, 1971.

Swett, Daniel. "Cultural Bias in the American Legal System", Law and Society Review IV (August, 1969), 79-110.

Tay, Alice. "Law in Communist China - Part I and II", The Sydney Law Review VI (1969), 335-370.

Timasheff, Nicholus. An Introduction to the Sociology of Law. Cambridge, Massachusetts: Harvard University Press, 1939.

_____. "Growth and Scope of Sociology of Law", in Becker, Howard and Boskoff, Alvin (eds.) Modern Sociological Theory in Continuity and Change. New York: The Dryden Press, 1957, Pp. 424-448.

Treves, R. et al. La Sociologia del Diritto. Milan: Communita, 1966.

_____ and Ferrari, V. (eds.) L'Insegnamento Sociologico del Diritto. Milan: Communita, 1976.

Turk, Austin. "Law as a Weapon in Social Conflict", Social Problems XXIII (February, 1976), 276-291.

Unger, Robert. Law in Modern Society: Toward A Criticism of Social Theory. New York: The Free Press, 1976.

Weber, Max. Law In Economy and Society. Cambridge, Massachusetts: Harvard University Press, 1954.

II. Sociology of Criminal Law

Carson, W.G. "The Sociology of Crime and the Emergence of Criminal Laws", in Rock, R. and McIntosh, M. (eds.) Deviance and Social Control. London: Tavistock, 1974, Pp.67-90.

Chambliss, William (ed.) Crime and the Legal Process. New York: McGraw-Hill Book Company, 1969.

_____ and Seidman, Robert. Law,
Order, and Power. Reading, Massachusetts:
Addison-Wesley Publishing Company, 1971.

_____. Functional and Conflict
Theories of Crime. New York: MSS Modular
Publications, 1973.

_____ (ed). Criminal Law in Action.
Santa Barbara, California: Hamilton
Publishing Company, 1975.

_____ and Mankoff, Milton (eds.)
Whose Law: What Order? New York: John
Wiley and Sons, 1976.

Dandurand, Yvon. "Public Opinion and the Crimin-
alization of Human Behavior: the Formulation of Criminal Definitions", paper presented to the Conference of the Research
Committee for the Sociology of Deviance and
Social Control.

Durkheim, Emile. Division of Labor in Society.
New York: Free Press, 1964.

Geis, Gilbert. "Sociology, Criminology, and
Criminal Law", Social Problems VII (1959),
40-46.

_____. "Jeremy Bentham" in Mannheim,
Hermann (ed.) Pioneers in Criminology.
Montclair, New Jersey: Patterson Smith,
1972, Pp. 53-66.

Gibbs, Jack. "Crime and the Sociology of Law", in
Knudten, Richard (ed.) Crime, Criminology,
and Contemporary Society. Homewood, Illinois:
The Dorsey Press, 1970, Pp. 397-404.

Gurvitch, Georges. Sociology of Law. London:
Routledge and Kegan Paul, 1947, Pp. 83-96.

Hills, Stuart. Crime, Power, and Morality: The
Criminal Law Process in the United States.
Scranton, Pennsylvania: Chandler Publishing
Company, 1971.

Jeffery, C. Ray. "Criminal Justice and Social
Change", in Davis, F. James et al. Society
and the Law. New York: Free Press, 1962,
Pp. 264-304.

_____. "The Historical Development
of Criminology", in Mannheim, Hermann (ed.)
Pioneers in Criminology. Montclair, New
Jersey: Patterson Smith, 1972, Pp. 459-498.

Lopez-Rey, Manuel. "Pedro Dorado Montero", in
Mannheim, Hermann (ed.) Pioneers in Crimin-
ology. Montclair, New Jersey: Patterson
Smith, 1972, Pp. 401-408.

Luden, Walter. "Emile Durkheim", in Mannheim,
Hermann (ed.) Pioneers in Criminology.
Montclair, New Jersey: Patterson Smith,
1972, Pp. 390-397.

Monachesi, Elio. "Cesare Beccaria", in Mannheim,
Hermann (ed.) Pioneers in Criminology.
Montclair, New Jersey: Patterson Smith, 1972,
Pp. 38-47.

Pepinsky, Harold. Crime and Conflict: A Study of
Law and Society. New York: Academic Press,
1976.

Quinney, Richard. Crime and Justice In Society.
Boston: Little, Brown and Company, 1969.

_____. Criminal Justice in America.
Boston: Little, Brown and Company, 1974.

Reasons, Charles. The Criminologist: Crime and
the Criminal. Pacific Palisades, California:
Goodyear Publishing Company, 1974.

_____. "Social Thought and Social
Structure: Competing Paradigms in Criminology", Criminology XIII (November, 1976),
332-365.

Rich, Robert M. "The Sociology of Criminal Law:
Toward a Paradigmatic Perspective", paper
presented at the American Society of Criminology Annual Meetings, November, 1976.

_____. "From Renner to Reasons: An
Analysis of Radical Theories of Criminology",
paper presented at the American Society of
Criminology Annual Meetings, November, 1976.

Schur, Edwin. Our Criminal Society. Englewood
Cliffs, New Jersey: Prentice-Hall, 1969.

Turk, Austin. Criminality and Legal Order.
Chicago: Rand McNally, 1969.

Vine, Margaret. "Gabriel Tarde", in Mannheim,
Hermann (ed.) Pioneers in Criminology.
Montclair, New Jersey: Patterson Smith,
1972, Pp. 292-302.

Vold, George. Theoretical Criminology. New York:
Oxford University Press, 1958.

III. Sociological Jurisprudence

Allen, Francis. The Borderland of Criminal
Justice: Essays in Law and Criminology.
Chicago: University of Chicago Press, 1964.

Angell, Robert. "The Value of Sociology to Law",
Michigan Law Review XXXI (1933), 512-525.

Aronson, Moses. "Cardozo's Doctrine of Sociological Jurisprudence", Journal of Social
Philosophy IV, number 3 (October, 1938), 5-44.

Berman, Harold and Greiner, William. The Nature
and Functions of Law. New York: The
Foundation Press, 1966.

Black, Donald. "The Boundaries of Legal Sociology", Yale Law Journal LXXXI June, 1972),
1086-1100.

Braybrooke, E.K. "The Sociological Jurisprudence of Roscoe Pound", in Sawer, Geoffrey (ed.) Studies in the Sociology of Law. Canberra: The Australian National University, 1961, Pp. 57-95.

Carbonnier, J. Sociologie Juridique. Paris: Colin, 1972.

Currie, Elliott. "Sociology of Law: The Unasked Questions", Yale Law Journal LXXXI (November, 1971), 134-147.

Feeley, Malcolm. "The Concept of Laws in Social Science: A Critique and Notes on an Expanded View", Law and Society Review X (Summer, 1976), 497-523.

Friedman, Lawrence. "Legal Rules and the Process of Social Change", Stanford Law Review XIX (April, 1967), 786-840.

_____. "Legal Culture and Social Development", Law and Society Review IV (August, 1969), 30-44.

Fuller, Lon. The Morality of Law. New Haven, Connecticut: Yale University Press, 1964.

Geis, Gilbert. "Sociology and Sociological Jurisprudence: Admixture of Law and Lore", Kentucky Law Journal LII (Winter, 1964), 267-293.

Gurvitch, Georges. Sociology of Law. London: Routledge and Kegan Paul, 1947, Pp. 130-144.

Hall, Jerome. Theft, Law and Society. Indianapolis, Indiana: The Bobbs-Merrill Company, 1952.

Hart, H.L.A. The Concept of Law. London: Oxford University Press, 1961.

Holmes, Oliver. "The Path of the Law", Harvard Law Review X (1897), 457-478.

Ladinsky, Jack. The Teaching of Law and Social
   Science Courses in the United States,
   Working Paper number 11, Center for Law and
   Behavioral Science, University of Wisconsin,
   Madison, June, 1974.

Llewellyn, Karl. Jurisprudence. Chicago:
   University of Chicago Press, 1962, Pp. 352-
   371.

Mohr, Hans et al. "The Scope of Interdisciplinary
   Collaboration", Osgoode Hall Law Journal VIII
   (1973), 373-378.

Nonet, Philippe. "For Jurisprudential Sociology",
   Law and Society Review X (Summer, 1976),
   525-545.

Podgorecki, Adam. "Law and Social Engineering",
   Human Organization XXI (Fall, 1962), 177-181.

Pound, Roscoe. "The Need for a Sociological
   Jurisprudence", The Green Bag XIX (October,
   1907), 607-615.

_____. "The Scope and Purpose of
   Sociological Jurisprudence (Parts I, II, and
   III)", Harvard Law Review XXIV-XXV (1911-
   1912, 489-516; 140-168; 591-619.)

Rich, Robert M. "Sociological Jurisprudence:
   Toward a Paradigmatic Perspective", un-
   published paper, 1975.

Stone, Julius. Law and the Social Sciences. St
   Paul, Minnesota: University of Minnesota
   Press, 1966.

Zeisel, Hans. "Sociology of Law, 1945-55", in
   Zetterberg, Hans (ed.) Sociology in the
   United States of America. New York: UNESCO,
   1956, Pp. 56-59.

IV. Anthropology of Law

Ball, Harry and Simpson, George. "Law and Social
    Change: Sumner Reconsidered", American
    Journal of Sociology LXVII (March, 1962),
    532-540.

Barnes, J.A. "Law as Politically Active: An
    Anthropological View", in Sawer, Geoffrey
    (ed.) Studies in the Sociology of Law.
    Canberra: The Australian National
    University, 1961, Pp. 167-193.

Bohannon, Paul. "Anthropology and the Law", in
    Tax, Saul (ed.) Horizons of Anthropology.
    Chicago: Aldine Publishing Company, 1964,
    Pp. 191-199.

_____. "The Differing Realms of the Law",
    The American Anthropologist LXVII, number 6
    December, 1965), 33-41.

Cairns, Huntington. "Law and Anthropology",
    Columbia Law Review XXXI (1931), 32-54.

_____. Law and the Social Sciences. New
    York: Harcourt, Brace and Company, 1935,
    Pp. 7-45.

Diamond, Arthur. Primitive Law. London: Watts
    and Company, 1935.

_____. The Evolution of Law and Order.
    Connecticut: Greenwood Press, 1951.

Diamond, Stanley. "The Rule of Law Versus the
    Order of Custom", Social Research XXXVIII
    (Spring, 1971), 42-72.

Gluckman, Max. "Concepts in the Comparative Study
    of Tribal Law", in Nader, Laura (ed.) Law in
    Culture and Society. Chicago: Aldine Pub-
    lishing Company, 1969, Pp. 349-373.

Henkin et al. "Law and Disorder Around the World:
    Other People's Problems", Columbia Journal
    of Law and Social Problems IX (1972), 63-87.

Hoebel, E. Adamson. The Law of Primitive Man.
Cambridge, Massachusetts: Harvard
University Press, 1967.

_____. "Law and Anthropology",
Virginia Law Review XXXII (1946), 835-853.

Lowie, Robert, "Anthropology and Law", in Ogburn,
W. and Goldenweiser, A. (eds.) The Social
Sciences and Their Interrelations. Boston:
Houghton Mifflin, 1927, Pp. 50-57.

_____. Primitive Society. New York:
Harper Torchbook, 1961, Pp. 397-425.

Llewellyn, Karl and Hoebel, E.A. The Cheyenne
Way: Conflict and Case Law in Primitive
Jurisprudence. Norman, Oklahoma: University
Of Oklahoma Press, 1941.

Maine, Henry. Ancient Law. Boston: Beacon
Press, 1956.

Malinowski, Bronislaw. Crime and Custom in
Savage Society. New York: Harcourt Brace
and Company, 1926.

_____. "Introduction", in Hogbin,
Herbert, Law and Order in Polynesia.
Connecticut: The Shoe String Press, 1961,
Pp. xix-lxxi.

Nader, Laura. "The Anthropological Study of Law",
The American Anthropologist LXVII, number 6
(December, 1965), 3-25.

_____. (ed.). Law in Culture and Society.
Chicago: Aldine Publishing Company, 1969.

Pospisil, Leopold. "Law and Order," in Clifton,
James (ed.) Introduction to Cultural Anthropology. Boston: Houghton Mifflin Company,
1968, Pp. 201-222.

Radcliffe-Brown, A.R. "Primitive Law", in
    Seligman, E. and Johnson, A. (eds.)
    Encyclopedia of the Social Sciences. New
    York: Macmillan Company, 1933, Pp. 202-
    206.

Redfield, Robert. "Primitive Law", University
    of Cincinnati Law Review XXXIII (Winter,
    1964), 1-12.

Rich, Robert M. "The Anthropology of Law:
    Toward a Paradigmatic Perspective", un-
    published paper, 1975.

Sumner, William. Folkways. Boston: Ginn and
    Company, 1906.

AUTHOR INDEX